TEACHER'S PET PUBLICATIONS

LITPLAN TEACHER PACK
for
Julius Caesar
based on the book by
William Shakespeare

Written by
Mary B. Collins

© 1997 Teacher's Pet Publications
All Rights Reserved

This **LitPlan** for William Shakespeare's
Julius Caesar
has been brought to you by Teacher's Pet Publications, Inc.

Copyright Teacher's Pet Publications 1997
11504 Hammock Point
Berlin MD 21811

Only the student materials in this LitPlan may be
reproduced. Pages such as worksheets and study
guides may be reproduced for use in the purchaser's
classroom. For any additional copyright questions,
contact Teacher's Pet Publications.

TABLE OF CONTENTS - *Julius Caesar*

Introduction	11
Unit Objectives	14
Reading Assignment Sheet	15
Unit Outline	16
Study Questions (Short Answer)	19
Quiz/Study Questions (Multiple Choice)	27
Pre-reading Vocabulary Worksheets	39
Lesson One (Introductory Lesson)	51
Oral Reading Evaluation Form	58
Writing Assignment 1	55
Writing Assignment 2	57
Writing Assignment 3	75
Writing Evaluation Form	74
Vocabulary Review Activities	67
Extra Writing Assignments/Discussion ?s	63
Unit Review Activities	77
Unit Tests	81
Unit Resource Materials	113
Vocabulary Resource Materials	127

ABOUT THE AUTHOR
WILLIAM SHAKESPEARE

SHAKESPEARE, William (1564-1616). For more than 350 years, William Shakespeare has been the world's most popular playwright. On the stage, in the movies, and on television his plays are watched by vast audiences. People read his plays again and again for pleasure. Students reading his plays for the first time are delighted by what they find.

Shakespeare's continued popularity is due to many things. His plays are filled with action, his characters are believable, and his language is thrilling to hear or read. Underlying all this is Shakespeare's deep humanity. He was a profound student of people and he understood them. He had a great tolerance, sympathy, and love for all people, good or evil.

While watching a Shakespearean tragedy, the audience is moved and shaken. After the show the spectators are calm, washed clean of pity and terror. They are saddened but at peace, repeating the old saying, "There, but for the grace of God, go I."

A Shakespearean comedy is full of fun. The characters are lively; the dialogue is witty. In the end young lovers are wed; old babblers are silenced; wise men are content. The comedies are joyous and romantic.

Boyhood in Stratford
William Shakespeare was born in Stratford-upon-Avon, England, in 1564. This was the sixth year of the reign of Queen Elizabeth I. He was christened on April 26 of that year. The day of his birth is unknown. It has long been celebrated on April 23, the feast of St. George. He was the third child and oldest son of John and Mary Arden Shakespeare. Two sisters, Joan and Margaret, died before he was born. The other children were Gilbert, a second Joan, Anne, Richard, and Edmund. Only the second Joan outlived William.

Shakespeare's father was a tanner and glovemaker. He was an alderman of Stratford for years. He also served a term as high bailiff, or mayor. Toward the end of his life John Shakespeare lost most of his money. When he died in 1601, he left William only a little real estate. Not much is known about Mary Shakespeare, except that she came from a wealthier family than her husband.

Stratford-upon-Avon is in Warwickshire, called the heart of England. In Shakespeare's day it was well farmed and heavily wooded. The town itself was prosperous and progressive. The town was proud of its grammar school. Young Shakespeare went to it, although when or for how long is not known. He may have been a pupil there between his 7th and 13th years. His studies must have been mainly in Latin. The schooling was good. All four schoolmasters at the school during Shakespeare's boyhood were graduates of Oxford University.

Nothing definite is known about his boyhood. From the content of his plays, he must have learned early about the woods and fields, about birds, insects, and small animals, about trades and outdoor sports, and about the country people he later portrayed with such good humor. Then and later he picked up an amazing stock of facts about hunting, hawking, fishing, dances, music, and other arts and sports. Among other subjects, he also learned about alchemy, astrology, folklore, medicine, and law. As good writers do, he collected information both from books and from daily observation of the world around him.

Marriage and Life in London
In 1582, when he was 18, he married Anne Hathaway. She was from Shottery, a village a mile from Stratford. Anne was seven or eight years older than Shakespeare. From this difference in their ages, a story arose that they were unhappy together. Their first daughter, Susanna, was born in 1583. In 1585 a twin boy and girl, Hamnet and Judith, were born.

What Shakespeare did between 1583 and 1592 is not known. Various stories are told. He may have taught school, worked in a lawyer's office, served on a rich man's estate, or traveled with a company of actors. One famous story says that about 1584 he and some friends were caught poaching on the estate of Sir Thomas Lucy of Carlecote, near Warwick, and were forced to leave town. A less likely story is that he was in London in 1588. There he was supposed to have held horses for theater patrons and later to have worked in the theaters as a callboy.

By 1592, however, Shakespeare was definitely in London and was already recognized as an actor and playwright. He was then 28 years old. In that year he was referred to in another man's book for the first time. Robert Greene, a playwright, accused him of borrowing from the plays of others.

Between 1592 and 1594, plague kept the London theaters closed most of the time. During these years Shakespeare wrote his earliest sonnets and two long narrative poems, 'Venus and Adonis' and 'The Rape of Lucrece'. Both were printed by Richard Field, a boyhood friend from Stratford. They were well received and helped establish him as a poet.

Shakespeare Prospers
Until 1598 Shakespeare's theater work was confined to a district northeast of London. This was outside the walls, in the parish of Shoreditch. Located there were two playhouses, the Theatre and the Curtain. Both were managed by James Burbage, whose son Richard Burbage was Shakespeare's friend and the greatest tragic actor of his day. Up to 1596 Shakespeare lived near these theaters in Bishopsgate, where the North Road entered the city. Sometime between 1596 and 1599, he moved across the Thames River to a district called Bankside. There, two theaters, the Rose and the Swan, had been built by Philip Henslowe. He was James Burbage's chief competitor in London as a theater manager.

The Burbages also moved to this district in 1598 and built the famous Globe Theatre. Its sign showed Atlas supporting the world-hence the theater's name. Shakespeare was associated with the Globe Theatre for the rest of his active life. He owned shares in it, which brought him much money.

Meanwhile, in 1597, Shakespeare had bought New Place, the largest house in Stratford. During the next three years he bought other property in Stratford and in London. The year before, his father, probably at Shakespeare's suggestion, applied for and was granted a coat of arms. It bore the motto Non sanz droict-Not without right. From this time on, Shakespeare could write "Gentleman" after his name. This meant much to him, for in his day actors were classed legally with criminals and vagrants.

Shakespeare's name first appeared on the title pages of his printed plays in 1598. In the same year Francis Meres, in 'Palladis Tamia: Wit's Treasury', praised him as a poet and dramatist. Meres's comments on 12 of Shakespeare's plays showed that Shakespeare's genius was recognized in his own time.

Honored As Actor and Playwright
Queen Elizabeth I died in 1603. King James I followed her to the throne. Shakespeare's theatrical company was taken under the king's patronage and called the King's Company. Shakespeare and the other actors were made officers of the royal household. The theatrical company was the most successful of its time. Before it was the King's Company, it had been known as the Earl of Derby's and the Lord Chamberlain's. In 1608 the company acquired the Blackfriars Theatre. This was a smaller and more aristocratic theater than the Globe. Thereafter the company alternated between the two playhouses.

Plays by Shakespeare were performed at both theaters, at the royal court, and in the castles of the nobles. After 1603 Shakespeare probably acted little, although he was still a good actor. His favorite roles seem to have been old Adam in 'As You Like It' and the Ghost in 'Hamlet'.

In 1607, when he was 43, he may have suffered a serious physical breakdown. In the same year his older daughter Susanna married John Hall, a doctor. The next year Shakespeare's first grandchild, Elizabeth, was born. Also in 1607 his brother Edmund, who had been an actor in London, died at the age of 27.

The Mermaid Tavern Group
About this time Shakespeare became one of the group of now-famous writers who gathered at the Mermaid Tavern in Cheapside. The club was formed by Sir Walter Raleigh. Ben Jonson was its leading spirit . Shakespeare was a popular member. He was admired for his talent and loved for his kindliness. Thomas Fuller, writing about 50 years later, gave an amusing account of the conversational duels between Shakespeare and Jonson: "Many were the wit-combats betwixt him and Ben Jonson; which two I behold like a Spanish great galleon and an English man-of-war; Master Jonson (like the former) was built far higher in learning; solid, but slow, in his performances. Shakespeare, with the English man-of-war, lesser in bulk, but lighter in sailing, could turn with all tides, tack about, and take advantage of all winds, by the quickness of his wit and invention."

Jonson sometimes criticized Shakespeare harshly. Nevertheless he later wrote a eulogy of Shakespeare that is remarkable for its feeling and acuteness. In it he said:

> Leave thee alone, for the comparison
> Of all that insolent Greece or haughty Rome
> Sent forth, or since did from their ashes come.
> Triumph, my Britain, thou hast one to show
> To whom all scenes of Europe homage owe.
> He was not of an age, but for all time!
> . . . .
> Sweet Swan of Avon! what a sight it were
> To see thee in our waters yet appear,
> And make those flights upon the banks of Thames,
> That so did take Eliza, and our James!

Death and Burial at Stratford

Shakespeare retired from his theater work in 1610 and returned to Stratford. His friends from London visited him. In 1613 the Globe Theatre burned. He lost much money in it, but he was still wealthy. He shared in the building of the new Globe. A few months before the fire he bought as an investment a house in the fashionable Blackfriars district of London.

On April 23, 1616, Shakespeare died at the age of 52. This date is according to the Old Style, or Julian, calendar of his time. The New Style, or Gregorian, calendar date is May 3, 1616. He was buried in the chancel of the Church of the Holy Trinity in Stratford. A stone slab-a reproduction of the original one, which it replaced in 1830-marks his grave. It bears an inscription, perhaps written by himself.

On the north wall of the chancel is his monument. It consists of a portrait bust enclosed in a stone frame. Below it is an inscription in Latin and English. This bust and the engraving by Martin Droeshout, prefixed to the First Folio edition of his plays (1623), are the only pictures of Shakespeare which can be accepted as showing his true likeness.

John Aubrey, an English antiquarian, wrote about Shakespeare 65 years after the poet's death. He evidently used information furnished by the son of one of Shakespeare's fellow actors. Aubrey described him as "a handsome, well-shaped man, very good company, and of a ready and pleasant smooth wit."

Shakespeare's will, still in existence, bequeathed most of his property to Susanna and her daughter. He left small mementoes to friends. He mentioned his wife only once, leaving her his "second best bed" with its furnishings. Much has been written about this odd bequest. There is little reason to think it was a slight. Indeed, it may have been a special mark of affection. The "second best bed" was probably the one they used. The best bed was reserved for guests. At any rate, his wife was entitled by law to one third of her husband's goods and real estate and to the use of their home for life. She died in 1623.

The will contains three signatures of Shakespeare. These, with three others, are the only known specimens of his handwriting in existence. Several experts also regard some lines in the manuscript of 'Sir Thomas More' as Shakespeare's own handwriting. He spelled his name in various ways. His father's papers show about 16 spellings. Shakspere, Shaxpere, and Shakespeare are the most common.

Did Shakespeare Really Write the Plays?
The outward events of Shakespeare's life are ordinary. He was hard-working, sober, and middle-class in his ways. He steadily gathered wealth and took good care of his family. Many people have found it impossible to believe that such a man could have written the plays. They feel that he could not have known such heights and depths of passion. They believe that the people around Shakespeare expressed little realization of his greatness. Some say that a man of his little schooling could not have learned about the professions, the aristocratic sports of hawking and hunting, the speech and manners of the upper classes.

Since the 1800's there has been a steady effort to prove that Shakespeare did not write the plays or that others did. For a long time the leading candidate was Sir Francis Bacon. Books on the Shakespeare-Bacon argument would fill a library,. After Bacon became less
popular, the Earl of Oxford and then other men were suggested as the authors. Nearly every famous Elizabethan was named. The most recent has been Christopher Marlowe. Some people even claim that "Shakespeare" is an assumed name for a whole group of poets and playwrights.

However, some men around Shakespeare-for example, Meres in 1598 and Jonson in 1623-did recognize his worth as a man and as a writer. To argue that an obscure Stratford boy could not have become the Shakespeare of literature is to ignore the mystery of genius. His knowledge is of the kind that could not be learned in school. It is the kind that only a genius could learn, by applying a keen intelligence to everyday life. Some great writers have had even less schooling than Shakespeare.

Few scholars take seriously these attempts to deprive Shakespeare of credit. Shakespeare's style is individual and cannot be imitated. Any good student recognizes it. It can be found nowhere else. Bacon is a poor candidate for the honor. Great as he was, he was certainly not a poet.

How the Plays Came Down to Us
Since the 1700's scholars have worked over the text of Shakespeare's plays. They have had to do so because the plays were badly printed, and no original manuscripts of them survive. In Shakespeare's day plays were not usually printed under the author's supervision. When a playwright sold a play to his company, he lost all rights to it. He could not sell it again to a publisher without the company's consent. When the play was no longer in demand on the
stage, the company itself might sell the manuscript. Plays were eagerly read by the Elizabethan

public. This was even more true during the plague years, when the theaters were closed. It was also true during times of business depression. Sometimes plays were taken down in shorthand and sold. At other times, a dismissed actor would write down the play from memory and sell it.

About half of Shakespeare's plays were printed during his lifetime in small, cheap pamphlets called quartos. Most of these were made from fairly accurate manuscripts. A few were in garbled form. In 1623, seven years after Shakespeare's death, his collected plays were published in a large, expensive volume called the First Folio. It contains all his plays except two of which he wrote only part-'Pericles' and 'Two Noble Kinsmen'. It also has the first engraved portrait of Shakespeare. This edition was authorized by Shakespeare's acting group, the King's Company. Some of the plays in it were printed from the accurate quartos and some from manuscripts in the theater. It is certain that many of these manuscripts were in Shakespeare's own handwriting. Others were copies. Still others, like the 'Macbeth' manuscript, had been revised by another dramatist.

Shakespearean scholars have been determining what Shakespeare actually wrote. They have done so by studying the language, stagecraft, handwriting, and printing of the period and by carefully examining and comparing the different editions. They have modernized spelling and punctuation, supplied stage directions, explained difficult passages, and made the plays easier for the modern reader to understand.

Another hard task has been to find out when the plays were written. About half of them have no definite date of composition. The plays themselves have been searched for clues. Other books have been examined. Scholars have tried to match events in Shakespeare's life with the subject matter of his plays. These scholars have used detective methods. They have worked with clues, deduction, shrewd reasoning, and external and internal evidence. External evidence consists of actual references in other books. Internal evidence is made up of verse tests and a study of the poet's imagery and figures of speech, which changed from year to year.

The verse tests follow the idea that a poet becomes more skillful with practice. Scholars long ago noticed that in his early plays Shakespeare used little prose, much rhyme, and certain types of rhythmical and metrical regularity. As he grew older he used more prose, less rhyme, and greater freedom and variety in rhythm and meter. From these facts, scholars have figured out the dates of those plays that had none.

Shakespeare As a Dramatist
The facts about Shakespeare are interesting in themselves, but they have little to do with his place in literature. Shakespeare wrote his plays to give pleasure. It is possible to spoil that pleasure by giving too much attention to his life, his times, and the problem of figuring out what he actually wrote. He can be enjoyed in book form, in the theater, or on television without our knowing any of these things.

Some difficulties stand in the way of this enjoyment. Shakespeare wrote more than 350 years ago. The language he used is naturally somewhat different from the language of today. Besides, he wrote in verse. Verse permits a free use of words that may not be understood by some readers. His plays are often fanciful. This may not appeal to matter-of-fact people who are used to modern realism. For all these reasons, readers may find him difficult. The worst handicap to enjoyment is the notion that Shakespeare is a "classic," a writer to be approached with awe.

The way to escape this last difficulty is to remember that Shakespeare wrote his plays for everyday people and that many in the audience were uneducated. They looked upon him as a funny, exciting, and lovable entertainer, not as a great poet. People today should read him as the people in his day listened to him. The excitement and enjoyment of the plays will banish most of the difficulties.

--- Courtesy of Compton's Learning Company

INTRODUCTION

This unit has been designed to develop students' reading, writing, thinking, and language skills through exercises and activities related to *Julius Caesar* by William Shakespeare. It includes twenty-two lessons, supported by extra resource materials.

The **introductory lessons** introduce students to background information about the play, Rome and the Roman Empire. Following the introductory activity, students are given a transition to explain how the activity relates to the play they are about to read. Following the transition, students are given the materials they will be using during the unit. At the end of the lesson, students begin the pre-reading work for the first reading assignment.

The **reading assignments** are approximately thirty pages each; some are a little shorter while others are a little longer. Students have approximately 15 minutes of pre-reading work to do prior to each reading assignment. This pre-reading work involves reviewing the study questions for the assignment and doing some vocabulary work for 8 to 10 vocabulary words they will encounter in their reading.

The **study guide questions** are fact-based questions; students can find the answers to these questions right in the text. These questions come in two formats: short answer or multiple choice. The best use of these materials is probably to use the short answer version of the questions as study guides for students (since answers will be more complete), and to use the multiple choice version for occasional quizzes. If your school has the appropriate equipment, it might be a good idea to make transparencies of your answer keys for the overhead projector.

The **vocabulary work** is intended to enrich students' vocabularies as well as to aid in the students' understanding of the book. Prior to each reading assignment, students will complete a two-part worksheet for approximately 8 to 10 vocabulary words in the upcoming reading assignment. Part I focuses on students' use of general knowledge and contextual clues by giving the sentence in which the word appears in the text. Students are then to write down what they think the words mean based on the words' usage. Part II nails down the definitions of the words by giving students dictionary definitions of the words and having students match the words to the correct definitions based on the words' contextual usage. Students should then have a thorough understanding of the words when they meet them in the text.

After each reading assignment, students will go back and formulate answers for the study guide questions. Discussion of these questions serves as a **review** of the most important events and ideas presented in the reading assignments.

After students complete reading the work, there is a **vocabulary review** lesson which pulls together all of the fragmented vocabulary lists for the reading assignments and gives students a review of all of the words they have studied.

Following the vocabulary review, a lesson is devoted to the **extra discussion questions/writing assignments**. These questions focus on interpretation, critical analysis and personal response, employing a variety of thinking skills and adding to the students' understanding of the novel.

The **group activity** which follows the discussion questions has students working in small groups to discuss the main themes of the novel. Using the information they have acquired so far through individual work and class discussions, students get together to further examine the text and to brainstorm ideas relating to the themes of the novel.

The group activity is followed by a **reports and discussion** session in which the groups share their ideas about the themes with the entire class; thus, the entire class is exposed to information about all of the themes and the entire class can discuss each theme based on the nucleus of information brought forth by each of the groups.

There are three **writing assignments** in this unit, each with the purpose of informing, persuading, or having students express personal opinions. The first assignment is to inform: students write a composition about the research work they have done. The second assignment is to persuade: students attempt to persuade the conspirators not to carry out their assassination plans. The third assignment is to give students a chance to simply express their own opinions: students give their opinions about what a "true and honorable wife" (spouse) would be.

In addition, there is a **nonfiction reading assignment**. Students are required to read a piece of nonfiction related in some way to *Julius Caesar* (articles about prejudice or coming of age, trial transcripts, etc.). After reading their nonfiction pieces, students will fill out a worksheet on which they answer questions regarding facts, interpretation, criticism, and personal opinions. During one class period, students make **oral presentations** about the nonfiction pieces they have read. This not only exposes all students to a wealth of information, it also gives students the opportunity to practice **public speaking**. In this unit the nonfiction reading assignment is tied in with the research assignment.

The **review lesson** pulls together all of the aspects of the unit. The teacher is given four or five choices of activities or games to use which all serve the same basic function of reviewing all of the information presented in the unit.

The **unit test** comes in two formats: multiple choice or short answer. As a convenience, two different tests for each format have been included. There is also an advanced short answer unit test for students who need a more challenging test.

There are additional **support materials** included with this unit. The **extra activities section** includes suggestions for an in-class library, crossword and word search puzzles related to the novel, and extra vocabulary worksheets. There is a list of **bulletin board ideas** which gives the teacher suggestions for bulletin boards to go along with this unit. In addition, there is a list of **extra class activities** the teacher could choose from to enhance the unit or as a substitution for an exercise the teacher might feel is inappropriate for his/her class. **Answer keys** are located directly after the **reproducible student materials** throughout the unit. The student materials may be reproduced for use in the teacher's classroom without infringement of copyrights. No other portion of this unit may be reproduced without the written consent of Teacher's Pet Publications, Inc.

The **level** of this unit can be varied depending upon the criteria on which the individual assignments are graded, the teacher's expectations of his/her students in class discussions, and the formats chosen for the study guides, quizzes and test. If teachers have other ideas/activities they wish to use, they can usually easily be inserted prior to the review lesson.

UNIT OBJECTIVES - *Julius Caesar*

1. Through reading William Shakespeare's Julius Caesar, students will gain a better understanding of the Roman Empire, Rome, and the assassination of Julius Caesar.

2. Students will demonstrate their understanding of the text on four levels: factual, interpretive, critical, and personal.

3. Students will look at Rome not only in the past but also in the present.

4. Students will see that political struggles for power within a government are a part of any historical era, not just in modern times.

5. Students will consider many quotations from the text to better appreciate Shakespeare's use of language and to better understand the play.

6. Students will be given the opportunity to practice reading aloud and silently to improve their skills in each area.

7. Students will answer questions to demonstrate their knowledge and understanding of the main events and characters in *Julius Caesar* as they relate to the author's theme development.

8. Students will enrich their vocabularies and improve their understanding of the play through the vocabulary lessons prepared for use in conjunction with the play.

9. The writing assignments in this unit are geared to several purposes:
    a. To have students demonstrate their abilities to inform, to persuade, or to express their own personal ideas
       NOTE: Students will demonstrate ability to write effectively to <u>inform</u> by developing and organizing facts to convey information. Students will demonstrate the ability to write effectively to <u>persuade</u> by selecting and organizing relevant information, establishing an argumentative purpose, and by designing an appropriate strategy for an identified audience. Students will demonstrate the ability to write effectively to <u>express personal ideas</u> by selecting a form and its appropriate elements.
    b. To check the students' reading comprehension
    c. To make students think about the ideas presented by the play
    d. To encourage logical thinking
    e. To provide an opportunity to practice good grammar and improve students' use of the English language.

READING ASSIGNMENT SHEET - *Julius Caesar*

Date Assigned	Reading Assignment	Completion Date
	Act I	
	Act II	
	Act III	
	Act IV	
	Act V	

UNIT OUTLINE - *Julius Caesar*

1 Group Assignment	2 Group Work	3 Reports	4 Introduction Materials Part Assignments PV Act I	5 Read Act I
6 ?s Act I Part Assignments PV Act II	7 Read Act II	8 ?s Act II Part Assignments PV Act III	9 Read Act III	10 ?s Act III Part Assignments PV Act IV
11 Read Act IV	12 ?s Act IV Part Assignments PV Act V	13 Read Act V ?s Act V	14 Vocabulary	15 Discussion
16 Writing Assignment 2	17 Group Activity	18 Reports & Discussion	19 Quotes	20 Writing Assignment 3
21 Review	22 Test			

Key: P = Preview Study Questions V = Vocabulary Work

STUDY GUIDE QUESTIONS

SHORT ANSWER STUDY GUIDE QUESTIONS - *Julius Caesar*

Below is a list of the characters of the play. Because there are so many, use this page to jot down some notes to remind you of each character's role in the play.

Flavius -
Marcellus -
Julius Caesar -
Casca -
Calpurnia -
Mark Antony -
Soothsayer -
Brutus -
Cassius -
Cicero -
Cinna -
Cinna (the poet) -
Lucius -
Decius -
Metellus -
Trebonius -
Portia -
Ligarius -
Publius -
Artemidorus -
Papilius -
Octavius -
Lepidus -
Pindarus -
Lucilius -
Messala -
Varro -
Claudius -
Titinius -
Cato -
Clitus -
Dardanius -
Volumnius -
Strato -

Julius Caesar Short Answer Study Guide Page 2

Act I
1. In Scene I, what do Flavius and Marcellus want the commoners to do?
2. What is the Soothsayer's advice to Caesar?
3. Explain the difference between the views of Caesar held by Cassius and Brutus.
4. Caesar clearly gives his thoughts about Cassius. What does he say?
5. Summarize Casca's explanation of why Caesar looked so sad.
6. At the end of Scene II in lines 312 - 326, Cassius makes plans. What plans does he make? Why?
7. Casca says, "For I believe they are portentous things/Unto the climate that they point upon." What does he mean?
8. Why does Cassius want Brutus to join the conspiracy?

Act II
1. To what decision does Brutus come in his orchard? Why?
2. What does Lucius give to Brutus in Scene I?
3. Why doesn't Brutus want to swear an oath with the conspirators?
4. For what reason does Metellus Cimber want Cicero to join the conspiracy?
5. Brutus is against including Cicero and against killing Mark Antony. Why?
6. Why did Brutus say, "Render me worthy of this noble wife!"?
7. Of what does Calpurnia try to convince Caesar?
8. Caesar yields to Calpurnia's wishes at first. Why does he change his mind and decide to go to the Senate meeting?
9. What does the note Artemidorus wants to give to Caesar say?

Act III
1. What is ironic about the timing of Caesar's murder (in relation to the preceding events)?
2. In the moments following Caesar's death, what do the conspirators proclaim to justify their deed?
3. Antony's servant brings a message to Brutus. What does he say?
4. Antony wants to speak at Caesar's funeral. What reaction does Brutus have? Cassius?
5. Under what conditions will Antony speak at the funeral?
6. What did Brutus say to the people at the funeral?
7. What did Antony say to the people at the funeral in his now famous "Friends, Romans, countrymen, lend me your ears" speech?
8. Why did Brutus and Cassius flee Rome?
9. What is the point of Act III Scene III?

Julius Caesar Short Answer Study Guide Page 3

Act IV
1. What did Antony, Octavius, and Lepidus gather to discuss?
2. To what does Antony compare Lepidus?
3. What problem has developed between Cassius and Brutus? How is it resolved?
4. What news did Messala bring Brutus?
5. For what reasons does Brutus want to lead his armies to Philippi?
6. What message did Caesar's ghost bring Brutus?

Act V
1. Why did Pindarus stab Cassius?
2. What causes Titinius to say, "The sun of Rome is set!"?
3. Who do the soldiers believe they have captured in Scene IV? Who is it really?
4. How does Brutus die?
5. Why did Antony say Brutus was the "noblest Roman of them all"?

ANSWER KEY: STUDY GUIDE QUESTIONS - *Julius Caesar*

Below is a list of the characters of the play. Because there are so many, use this page to jot down some notes to remind you of each character's role in the play.

Flavius - tribune who breaks up crowd waiting to honor Caesar's triumph
Marcellus - tribune who breaks up crowd waiting to honor Caesar's triumph
Julius Caesar - Emperor of Rome
Casca - first to stab Caesar
Calpurnia - Caesar's wife
Mark Antony - devoted follower of Caesar; defeats Brutus
Soothsayer - warns Caesar to "Beware the Ides of March"
Brutus - joins and then leads the conspiracy to kill Caesar
Cassius - organizes the conspiracy and gets Brutus to join
Cicero - Roman Senator Casca to whom talks on the eve of the assassination
Cinna - plants the forged letter for Cassius, also a conspirator
Cinna (the poet) - mistaken for Cinna the conspirator
Lucius - servant to Brutus
Decius - reinterprets Calpurnia's dream and convinces Caesar to go to Senate
Metellus - distracts Caesar's attention so conspirators can carry out their plan
Trebonius - takes Antony away from the assassination scene so he won't interfere
Portia - wife of Brutus
Ligarius - vows to follow Brutus
Publius - one of many who escort Caesar to the Senate meeting
Artemidorus - gives Caesar a letter of warning naming the conspirators
Papilius - wishes Cassius well in his "enterprise"
Octavius - heir of Julius Caesar
Lepidus - joins with Octavius and Antony, used by Octavius and Antony
Pindarus - servant to Cassius
Lucilius - captured by Antony's soldiers, mistaken for Brutus
Messala - reports Portia's death, discovers Cassius' body
Varro - servant of Brutus
Claudius - servant of Brutus
Titinius - officer, guards tent at Sardis
Cato - soldier in army of Brutus and Cassius
Clitus - servant of Brutus, refused to kill Brutus
Dardanius - servant of Brutus, refused to kill Brutus
Volumnius - friend and soldier to Brutus, refuses to hold Brutus' sword
Strato - holds Brutus' suicide sword

Act I

1. In Scene I, what do Flavius and Marcellus want the commoners to do?
    They want the commoners to break up and move along; they don't want them to celebrate Caesar's triumphs.

2. What is the Soothsayer's advice to Caesar?
    The Soothsayer told Caesar to "Beware the Ides of March."

3. Explain the difference between the views of Caesar held by Cassius and Brutus.
    Cassius openly wants Caesar out of power. He is jealous and wants better for himself. Brutus has been thinking about Caesar and the state of his countrymen, and at this point is ready to listen to Cassius. Although Brutus loves Caesar, he recognizes Caesar's flaws.

4. Caesar clearly gives his thoughts about Cassius. What does he say?
    Caesar says that Cassius "has a lean and hungry look. He thinks too much and such men are dangerous."

5. Summarize Casca's explanation of why Caesar looked so sad.
    Antony offered Caesar a crown. When he refused it, the crowd cheered. So, although Caesar really wanted the crown, he at that point could not publicly accept it. Then he had a seizure.

6. At the end of Scene II in lines 312 - 326, Cassius makes plans. What plans does he make? Why?
    He is going to forge notes to Brutus from several citizens in order to help sway Brutus against Caesar.

7. Casca says, "For I believe they are portentous things/Unto the climate that they point upon." What does he mean?
    He thinks the list of "unnatural" sights he has just told Cicero about are signs of the tragedy about to unfold in their country.

8. Why does Cassius want Brutus to join the conspiracy?
    Brutus is a favorite of the people. He is honorable and well-thought-of. If the people would see that Brutus supported the conspiracy, the conspirators would be in better favor with the people following the assassination.

Act II

1. To what decision does Brutus come in his orchard? Why?
    He decides to join the conspiracy to murder Caesar. He believes after Caesar is crowned, he will abuse his power, so Brutus thinks it best to "kill him in the shell; that is, to murder him before he gets a chance to abuse his power.

2. What does Lucius give to Brutus in Scene I?
   He brings the forged note which had been thrown through Brutus' window.

3. Why doesn't Brutus want to swear an oath with the conspirators?
   He thinks a just cause needs no oath to bind the doers to their cause.

4. For what reason does Metellus Cimber want Cicero to join the conspiracy?
   ". . . his silver hairs/Will purchase us a good opinion,/And buy men's voices to commend our deeds. . . ."

5. Brutus is against including Cicero and against killing Mark Antony. Why?
   He says Cicero will not follow any plan started by someone else. Killing Mark Antony isn't necessary; it would be too bloody.

6. Why did Brutus say, "Render me worthy of this noble wife!"?
   Portia has shown her concern for him and insists on sharing his emotional burden.

7. Of what does Calpurnia try to convince Caesar?
   She tries to convince him that her dreams are omens of tragedy and that he should not go to the Senate meeting.

8. Caesar yields to Calpurnia's wishes at first. Why does he change his mind and decide to go to the Senate meeting?
   Decius reinterprets Calpurnia's dream to entice Caesar to go to the meeting.

9. What does the note Artemidorus wants to give to Caesar say?
   It warns Caesar about the conspiracy and names the conspirators.

Act III
1. What is ironic about the timing of Caesar's murder (in relation to the preceding events)?
   He has just finished saying how he is one who is as "constant as the Northern Star" and comparing himself to Olympus. He is destroyed just after proclaiming his magnificence and indestructibility.

2. In the moments following Caesar's death, what do the conspirators proclaim to justify their deed?
   "Liberty! Freedom! Tyranny is dead!"

3. Antony's servant brings a message to Brutus. What does he say?
   Antony praises Brutus for being honest and noble and requests to be able to safely come see Brutus to hear why Caesar was murdered.

4. Antony wants to speak at Caesar's funeral. What reaction does Brutus have? Cassius?
    Brutus would let him speak. Cassius thinks it is too dangerous for them to let Antony speak to the people.

5. Under what conditions will Antony speak at the funeral?
    He will be allowed to speak if he doesn't blame the conspirators, admits he speaks by their permission, and speaks last (after Brutus).

6. What did Brutus say to the people at the funeral?
    He said he loved Caesar, but he loved Rome more. He asked them if they would "rather Caesar were living and die all slaves then that Caesar were dead, to live all freemen." He asked for anyone he had offended to step forth. (No one did.) Brutus attempted to appeal to the crowd's reason, to show them that the assassination was the only logical way to do the best thing for the people.

7. What did Antony say to the people at the funeral in his now famous "Friends, Romans, countrymen, lend me your ears" speech?
    Antony called the conspirators "honorable men" and does not obviously attempt to degrade the crowd's new-found heroes. Instead, he begins pointing our examples of Caesar's behavior which clearly contradict the accusations made by the conspirators. He notes that Caesar shared the spoils of war, showed compassion for the common people, and denied acceptance of the crown three times. These were not deeds of an ambitious man, so Antony said. Throughout the speech, he masterfully manipulates the crowd's emotions until, at the end, they praise him and Caesar and are ready to riot.

8. Why did Brutus and Cassius flee Rome?
    Their lives were in danger after Antony's remarks at the funeral.

9. What is the point of Act III Scene III?
    It graphically shows the violent mood of the crowd. Even when told they have the wrong Cinna, they want to destroy him anyway for his bad verses and for having the same name as Cinna the conspirator.

Act IV
1. What did Antony, Octavius and Lepidus gather to discuss?
    They were deciding which Romans should live or die. They wanted to eliminate anyone who could cause them trouble.

2. To what does Antony compare Lepidus?
    He compares him to his own horse and calls him an animal to be trained and used.

3. What problem has developed between Cassius and Brutus? How is it resolved?
   Cassius was offended that Brutus did not seriously consider his letters on behalf of Lucius Pella. Brutus said Cassius should not have written on behalf of such a man and he goes on to accuse Cassius of accepting bribes himself. It is resolved (after a great deal of name-calling and threats to fight) by the end of their conversation. Brutus basically holds to his position and lets Cassius talk himself out.

4. What news did Messala bring Brutus?
   He brought news that Antony, Octavius and Lepidus have had a hundred Senators killed and that Portia also is dead.

5. For what reasons does Brutus want to lead his armies to Philippi?
   (a) They can gather fresh forces as they march to Philippi (b) That the enemy is increasing and his army is at a high point ready to decline, and (c) They are on a "tide" of "fortune" and should strike while they are on a good tide.
   (Note that it is ironic that Brutus' decision to move early is the key to his defeat. If he had waited, the outcome may have been different.)

6. What message did Caesar's ghost bring Brutus?
   He said he would see Brutus at Philippi.

Act V

1. Why did Pindarus stab Cassius?
   Cassius ordered Pindarus to kill Cassius after he believes Titanius has been captured by the enemy. (Note the irony that Titanius was in fact NOT captured; rather, he was being congratulated by his own side.)

2. What causes Titinius to say, "The sun of Rome is set!"?
   He learns of Cassius' death.

3. Who do the soldiers believe they have captured in Scene IV? Who is it really?
   They believe they have captured Brutus, but they have actually captured Lucilius.

4. How does Brutus die?
   Brutus runs on his own sword. He recognizes defeat and refuses to give Antony the "honor" of killing him.

5. Why did Antony say Brutus was the "noblest Roman of them all"?
   All the other conspirators killed Caesar of envy or for personal gain. Brutus truly believed he was doing the right thing for his countrymen.

MULTIPLE CHOICE STUDY GUIDE/QUIZ QUESTIONS - *Julius Caesar*

Act I
1. In Scene I, what do Flavius and Marcellus want the commoners to do?
    A. Go home and put on their best clothes.
    B. Stand along the sides of the street to get ready for Caesar's procession.
    C. Break up, move along, and ignore Caesar's victory.
    D. Offer their services free of charge to Caesar.

2. What is the Soothsayer's advice to Caesar?
    A. "Neither a borrower nor a lender be."
    B. "Beware the Ides of March."
    C. "Go you down that way towards the Capitol."
    D. "Make haste, for it grows very late."

3. Explain the difference between the views of Caesar held by Cassius and Brutus.
    A. Cassius openly wants Caesar out of power. Brutus loves Caesar but recognizes his flaws and thinks about the state of his countrymen.
    B. Cassius wants Caesar to stay in power. Brutus thinks Cassius would be a\ better leader and wants to help him take over.
    C. Cassius wants Caesar out of power. Brutus agrees but thinks Cassia would not be a good leader either.
    D. Cassius thinks Caesar should share his power with Cassius, Brutus and others. Brutus thinks the power should be divided equally among all of the countrymen.

4. Caesar clearly gives his thoughts about Cassius. What does he say?
    A. "It doth amaze me
       A man of such feeble temper should
       So get the start of a majestic world."
    B. "He had rather be a villager
       Than to repute himself a son of Rome."
    C. "He has a lean and hungry look.;
       He thinks too much. Such men are dangerous."
    D. "We have both fed as well, and we can both
       Endure the winter's cold as well as he."

5. What is Casca's explanation of Caesar's sad look? (Act I)
    A. He is suffering from battle fatigue and lack of proper food.
    B. He really wants the crowd, but the crowd cheered when he refused it.
    C. He does not like public ceremonies and wants to go home.
    D. The crowd begs him to accept the crown, but he does not want it.

Caesar Multiple Choice Study Questions Page 2

6. At the end of Scene II in lines 312 - 326, Cassius makes plans. What plans does he make? Why?
    A. He is going to ask Casca and Brutus to have dinner with him the following evening to discuss what to do about Caesar.
    B. He plans to hold a reception in Caesar's honor to make amends with him.
    C. He is going to forge notes to Brutus from several citizens in order to help sway Brutus against Caesar.
    D. He is going to forge notes from Brutus to Caesar.

7. Casca says, "For I believe they are portentous things/Unto the climate that they point upon." What does he mean?
    A. He thinks they are going to continue to have bad weather.
    B. He thinks Caesar has caused some kind of magic spell to be put upon the city.
    C. He thinks the "unnatural" sights he has seen are signs of tragedy about to unfold in his country.
    D. He thinks Caesar will make some needed improvements in the way the government is run.

8. Why does Cassius want Brutus to join the conspiracy?
    A. Brutus is well thought of by the people. If he supported the conspiracy, the conspirators would be in better favor with the people following the assassination.
    B. Brutus has the best knowledge of the layout of the Capitol. It would be easy for him to plan a secret attack.
    C. Brutus has great influence over the soldiers. Cassius needs Brutus to direct them not to help Caesar.
    D. Brutus is very wealthy. They will need a lot of money to set up the new government.

Caesar Multiple Choice Study Questions Page 3

Act II

9. To what decision does Brutus come in his orchard? Why?
    A. He decides to stay loyal to Caesar and to warn him of the conspirators' plot because he believes that Caesar has Rome's best interests at heart.
    B. He decides to remain neutral because he does not fully trust the conspirators or Caesar.
    C. He decides to join the conspiracy to murder Caesar because he thinks Caesar will abuse his power if he is crowned.
    D. He decides to leave the city and go into hiding.

10. What does Lucius give to Brutus in Scene I?
    A. He brings the forged note that has been thrown through the window.
    B. He brings Brutus a cup of wine to ease his troubled sleep.
    C. He brings a note from Caesar asking him to come to the palace.
    D. He brings a plate of eggs for breakfast.

11. Why doesn't Brutus want to swear an oath with the conspirators?
    A. He is planning to double-cross them later on.
    B. He thinks it is bad luck to swear an oath.
    C. He is afraid Lucius will overhear him and run to warn Caesar.
    D. He thinks a just cause needs no oath to bind the doers to their cause.

12. For what reason does Metellus Cimber want Cicero to join the conspiracy?
    A. "... for his is given
       To sports, to wildness and much company.
       There is no fear in him..."
    B. "...his silver hairs
       Will purchase us a good opinion.
       And buy men's voices to commend our deeds..."
    C. "...we shall find of him
       A shrewd contriver..."
    D. "...thy master is wise and valiant Roman..."

13. Brutus is against including Cicero and against killing Mark Antony. Why?
    A. Cicero is a coward, and Mark Antony can be persuaded to side with them.
    B. Cicero will not follow any plan started by someone else, and killing Mark Antony would be too bloody.
    C. Cicero may be a spy of Caesar's, and Mark Antony will not be a threat once Caesar is dead.
    D. Cicero wants the crown for himself, and if they kill Mark Antony, the Army will retaliate.

Caesar Multiple Choice Study Questions Page 4

14. Why did Brutus say, "Render me worthy of this noble wife!"?
    A. He feels badly. He knows he has not been attentive to his wife lately.
    B. He wants to keep his plan a secret from his wife because she will be angry.
    C. Portia has shown her concern for him and insists on sharing his emotional burden.
    D. Portia approves of his plan and offers to help.

15. Of what does Calpurnia try to convince Caesar?
    A. Her dreams are omens of tragedy, and he should not go to the Senate meeting.
    B. Her spies have told her that there is a plot against Caesar.
    C. There is going to be a terrible earthquake, and he should cancel the Senate meeting.
    D. He should let her and the other wives be present for his coronation.

16. Caesar yields to Calpurnia's wishes at first. Why does he change his mind and decide to go to the Senate meeting?
    A. His servants tell him the priests said it was alright for him to go.
    B. He knows that his army is strong and will protect him.
    C. He has seen a good luck omen in the sky. He thinks it is stronger than Calpurnia's dreams.
    D. Decius reinterprets Calpurnia's dream to entice Caesar to go to the meeting.

17. What does the note Artemidorus wants to give to Caesar say?
    A. It is a speech for Caesar to deliver at the coronation.
    B. It is a letter from Calpurnia. She apologizes and sends her love.
    C. It warns Caesar of the Conspiracy and names the conspirators.
    D. It is a note from one of the senators who will not be at the meeting.

Caesar Multiple Choice Study Questions Page 5

Act III

18. What is ironic about the timing of Caesar's murder (in relation to the preceding events)?
    A. He is murdered just as he is reading the warning from Portia.
    B. He is destroyed just after proclaiming his magnificence and indestructibility.
    C. It occurs just after a great storm and earthquake.
    D. Brutus has changed his mind but is not able to stop the others.

19. In the moments following Caesar's death, what do the conspirators proclaim to justify their deed?
    A. "Life! Liberty! The pursuit of happiness!"
    B. "Et tu, Brute!"
    C. "Fates, we will know your pleasures."
    D. "Liberty! Freedom! Tyranny is dead!"

20. Antony's servant brings a message to Brutus. What does he say?
    A. Antony praises Brutus for being honest and requests to be able to safely see Brutus to hear why Caesar was murdered.
    B. Antony expresses his anger and vows that Caesar's murder shall be avenged.
    C. Antony surrenders and asks for safe passage from the city.
    D. Antony congratulates Brutus and says he is glad Caesar is dead.

21. Antony wants to speak at Caesar's funeral. What reaction does Brutus have? Cassius?
    A. They both refuse.
    B. Brutus agrees, but Cassius thinks it is dangerous to let Antony speak to the people.
    C. Brutus refuses, but Cassius thinks it will calm the people.
    D. They both agree that it will help their cause.

22. Under what conditions will Antony speak at the funeral?
    A. He must go first, take full responsibility for his speech, and swear allegiance to Brutus.
    B. He must use the speech that the conspirators have written and say that he approves of their actions.
    C. He must speak after Casca and only wish Caesar eternal peace.
    D. He must not blame the conspirators, admit he speaks by their permission, and speak last, after Brutus.

Caesar Multiple Choice Study Questions Page 6

23. What did Brutus say to the people at the funeral?
    A. He told them the assassination was the only logical way to do the best thing for the people.
    B. He told them he would be a much better ruler than Caesar and asked for their trust and support.
    C. He said he would divide Caesar's wealth among the people after the funeral.
    D. He criticized Caesar for being a cruel and evil ruler.

24. What did Antony say to the people at the funeral in his now famous "Friends, Romans, countrymen, lend me your ears" speech?
    A. He accuses the conspirators of treason and demands that they be put to death for Caesar's murder.
    B. He says the Caesar deserved to die and the people should thank the conspirators.
    C. He contradicts the accusations made by the conspirators of treason and demands that they be put to death for Caesar's murder.
    D. He praises Caesar and asks that a memorial be built for him.

25. Why did Brutus and Cassius flee Rome?
    A. They had hidden Caesar's fortune and wanted to recover it.
    B. They went to get the army to put down the riot.
    C. They were following their wives, who had left the city earlier.
    D. Their lives were in danger after Antony's remarks at the funeral.

26. What is the point of Act III Scene III?
    A. It graphically shows the violent mood of the crowd.
    B. It shows the people's dislike of bad poetry.
    C. It lets us know what Brutus is thinking.
    D. It encourages sympathy for Mark Antony.

Caesar Multiple Choice Study Questions Page 7

Act IV

27. What did Antony, Octavius, and Lepidus gather to discuss?
 A. The date and agenda of the next Senate meeting.
 B. They were deciding which potential troublemakers to kill.
 C. They were making plans for the coronation of Brutus.
 D. They were planning their escape from the city.

28. To what does Antony compare Lepidus?
 A. To a god to be worshipped
 B. To a woman to be pitied for her cowardice
 C. To a horse to be trained and used
 D. To a brave and fierce warrior.

29. What problem has developed between Cassius and Brutus? How is it resolved?
 A. Cassius is offended that Brutus did not seriously consider his letters on behalf of Lucius Pella. Brutus accuses Cassius of accepting bribes. Brutus holds to his position.
 B. Cassius wanted to head the army. Brutus does not think he would be a competent leader. It is resolved when Cassius gives in to Brutus.
 C. Brutus has demanded a large amount of gold from Cassius. At first Cassius refuses, but then he reluctantly gives in to Brutus's demands for the good of Rome.
 D. Brutus wants to return to Rome immediately. Cassius thinks they should wait until the people's anger dies down. They finally agree to wait.

30. What news did Messala bring Brutus?
 A. The rioting has stopped and it is safe for them to return to the city.
 B. Antony has fled and the city is in turmoil.
 C. Antony, Octavius, and Lepidus have had a hundred Senators killed, and Portia is also dead.
 D. Portia has left the city and gone into hiding. A loyal faction is working to ensure a safe return for her and for Brutus and Cassius.

31. Which of these is not a reason that Brutus wants to lead his armies to Philippi?
 A. They can gather fresh forces as their march toward Philippi.
 B. The enemy is increasing, and his army is at a high point ready to decline.
 C. They are on a "tide" of "fortune" and should strike while they are on a good tide.
 D. Antony is not expecting Brutus to go to Philippi. Brutus will have the element of surprise on his side.

Caesar Multiple Choice Study Questions Page 8

32. What message did Caesar's ghost bring Brutus?
    A. Beware the Ides of March.
    B. He would see Brutus at Philippi.
    C. Brutus would never live to rule Rome.
    D. Brutus should not go to Philippi but should go directly to Rome.

Caesar Multiple Choice Study Questions Page 9

Act V

33. Why did Pindarus stab Cassius?
    A. He was angry because Cassius had helped kill Caesar.
    B. He had secretly changed sides and had been ordered to do so by Antony.
    C. Cassius asked him to do it when they thought Titinius had been captured by the enemy.
    D. Pindarus is afraid that Cassius will try to take over, and he wants Brutus to rule.

34. What causes Titinius to say, "The sun of Rome is set!"?
    A. He sees Rome burning in the distance.
    B. He thinks they will soon be defeated.
    C. He can tell that night is approaching and the fighting will have to wait for morning.
    D. He learns that Cassius is dead.

35. Who do the soldiers believe they have captured in Scene IV? Who is it really?
    A. They think it is Brutus, but it is actually Lucilius.
    B. They think it is Cassius, but it is actually Cato.
    C. They think it is Lucilius, but it is actually Messala.
    D. They think it is Titinius, but it is actually Pindarus.

36. How does Brutus die?
    A. Antony kills him in a fight.
    B. He kills himself with his sword.
    C. The ghost of Caesar frightened him to death.
    D. He is taken prisoner and one of the soldiers accidentally kills him.

37. Why did Antony say Brutus was the "noblest Roman of them all"?
    A. Brutus was the only one who died an honorable death.
    B. Brutus saw the error of his ways before he died and apologized to Antony.
    C. The others killed Caesar for personal gain, but Brutus believed he was doing the right thing for his countrymen.
    D. Antony was trying to appease the people so they would not riot when they learned Brutus was dead.

ANSWER KEY - MULTIPLE CHOICE STUDY/QUIZ QUESTIONS
Julius Caesar

Multiple Choice
1. C
2. B
3. A
4. C
5. B
6. C
7. C
8. A
9. C
10. A
11. D
12. B
13. B
14. C
15. A
16. D
17. C
18. B
19. D
20. A
21. B
22. D
23. A
24. C
25. D
26. A
27. B
28. C
29. A
30. C
31. D
32. B
33. C
34. D
35. A
36. B
37. C

PREREADING VOCABULARY WORKSHEETS

VOCABULARY - *Julius Caesar*

Act I
Part I: Using Prior Knowledge and Contextual Clues

Below are the sentences in which the vocabulary words appear in the text. Read the sentence. Use any clues you can find in the sentence combined with your prior knowledge, and write what you think the underlined words mean on the lines provided.

1. But let not therefore my good friends be grieved --
   Among which number, Cassius, be you one --
   Nor <u>construe</u> any further my neglect
   Than that poor Brutus, with himself at war,
   Forgets the shows of love to other men.

   _____

2. Thoughts of great value, worthy <u>cogitations</u>

   _____

3. Upon the word,
   <u>Accoutered</u> as I was, I plunged in
   And bade him follow.

   _____

4. How I have thought of this and of these times,
   I shall recount hereafter; for this present,
   I would not, so with love I might <u>entreat</u> you,
   Be any further moved.

   _____

5. I saw Mark Antony offer him a crown, yet 'twas not a crown neither, 'twas one of these
   coronets; and, as I told you, he put it by once. But for all that, to my thinking, he would <u>fain</u>
   have had it.

   _____

6. What a blunt fellow is this grown to be!
   He was quick <u>mettle</u> when he went to school.

   _____

Julius Caesar Act I Continued

7. When these <u>prodigies</u>
    Do so conjointly meet, let not men say
    "These are their reasons, they are natural."

_____

8. For I believe they are <u>portentous</u> things
    Unto the climate that they point upon.

_____

Part II: Determining the Meaning
    You have tried to figure out the meanings of the vocabulary words for Act I. Now match the vocabulary words to their dictionary definitions. If there are words for which you cannot figure out the definition by contextual clues and by process of elimination, look them up in a dictionary.

    ___ 1. construe   A. omens
    ___ 2. cogitations   B. fully armed
    ___ 3. accoutered   C. interpret
    ___ 4. entreat   D. temperament
    ___ 5. fain   E. foreboding
    ___ 6. mettle   F. thoughts
    ___ 7. prodigies   G. make an earnest request of
    ___ 8. portentous   H. gladly

Vocabulary - *Julius Caesar* Act II

Part I: Using Prior Knowledge and Contextual Clues
    Below are the sentences in which the vocabulary words appear in the text. Read the sentence. Use any clues you can find in the sentence combined with your prior knowledge, and write what you think the underlined words mean on the lines provided.

1. And since the quarrel
   Will bear no color for the thing he is,
   Fashion it thus: that what he is <u>augmented</u>,
   Would run to these and these extremities.

   _____

2. Where wilt thou find a cavern dark enough
   To mask thy monstrous <u>visage</u>? Seek none, Conspiracy ---
   Hide it in smiles and <u>affability</u>

   _____

3. Yet I fear him,/For in the <u>ingrafted</u> love he bears to Caesar---

   _____

4. But it is doubtful yet
   Whether Caesar will come forth today or no,
   For he is superstitious grown of late,
   Quite from the main opinion he held once
   Of Fantasy, of dreams and ceremonies.
   It may be these apparent <u>prodigies</u>,
   And the persuasion of his <u>augurers</u>,
   May hold him from the Capitol today.

   _____

5. Is it excepted I should know no secrets
   That <u>appertain</u> to you?

   _____

41

Vocabulary - *Julius Caesar* Act II Continued

6. My heart laments that virtue cannot live
   Out of the teeth of <u>emulation</u>.

_____

Part II: Determining the Meaning: Match the definitions to the vocabulary words.

___ 9. augmented   A. planted firmly; established
___ 10. visage   B. made greater in size, extent or quantity
___ 11. affability   C. envy
___ 12. ingrafted   D. signs of disaster
___ 13. prodigies   E. face
___ 14. augurers   F. belong to as a proper function or part
___ 15. appertain   G. professional interpreters of omens
___ 16. emulation   H. friendliness; graciousness

Vocabulary - *Julius Caesar* Act III

Part I: Using Prior Knowledge and Contextual Clues

Below are the sentences in which the vocabulary words appear in the text. Read the sentence. Use any clues you can find in the sentence combined with your prior knowledge, and write what you think the underlined words mean on the lines provided.

1. Most high, most mighty, and most <u>puissant</u> Caesar,
   Metellus Cimber throws before thy seat
   A humble heart----

   _____

2. Our arms in strength of <u>malice</u>, and our hearts
   Of brothers' temper, do receive you in
   With all kind love, good thoughts, and reverence.

   _____

3. Only be patient till we have <u>appeased</u>
   The multitude, beside themselves with tear,
   And then we will deliver you the cause
   Why I, that did love Caesar when I struck him
   Have thus proceeded.

   _____

4. Domestic fury and fierce civil <u>strife</u>
   Shall cumber all the parts of Italy.

   _____

5. There shall I try,
   In my <u>oration</u>, how the people take
   The cruel issue of these bloody men,
   According to the which, thou shalt discourse
   To young Octavius of the state of things.

   _____

6. Who is here so <u>base</u> that would be a bondman?

   _____

Julius Caesar Act III Continued

7. He hath brought many captives to Rome,
   Whose ransoms did the general <u>coffers</u> fill.

   _____

8. You all do know this <u>mantle</u>. I remember
   The first time ever Caesar put it on.

   _____

9. I am not Cinna the <u>conspirator</u>.

   _____

Part II: Determining the Meaning
    You have tried to figure out the meanings of the vocabulary words for Act III. Now match the vocabulary words to their dictionary definitions. If there are words for which you cannot figure out the definition by contextual clues and by process of elimination, look them up in a dictionary.

___ 17. puissant	A. struggle, fight or quarrel
___ 18. malice	B. formal speech
___ 19. appeased	C. cloak
___ 20. strife	D. one who plans with others to commit an illegal act
___ 21. oration	E. powerful; mighty
___ 22. base	F. public treasury
___ 23. coffers	G. soothed; pacified
___ 24. mantle	H. ill-will or spite
___ 25. conspirator	I. devoid of high values or ethics

Vocabulary - *Julius Caesar* Acts IV and V

Part I: Using Prior Knowledge and Contextual Clues
    Below are the sentences in which the vocabulary words appear in the text. Read the sentence. Use any clues you can find in the sentence combined with your prior knowledge, and write what you think the underlined words mean on the lines provided.

1. But, Lepidus, go you to Caesar's house.
   Fetch the will hither, and we shall determine
   How to cut off some charge in <u>legacies</u>.

_____

2. The name of Cassius honors this corruption,
   And <u>chastisement</u> doth therefore hide his head.

_____

3. When Marcus Brutus grows so <u>covetous</u>,
   To lock such rascal counters from his friends,
   Be ready, gods, with all your thunderbolts,
   Dash him to pieces!

_____

4. Why do you cross me in this <u>exigent</u>?

_____

5. Coming from Sardis, on our former <u>ensign</u>
   Two mighty eagles fell, and there they perched

_____

6. Thou never comest unto a happy birth,
   But kill'st the mother that <u>engendered</u> thee!

_____

Julius Caesar Acts IV and V Continued

7. For piercing steel and darts <u>envenomed</u>
   Shall be as welcome to the ears of Brutus
   As tidings of this sight.

_____

8. Oh, Julius Caesar, thou art mighty yet!
   Thy spirit walks abroad, and turns our swords
   In our own proper <u>entrails</u>.

_____

Part II: Determining the Meaning
   You have tried to figure out the meanings of the vocabulary words for Chapters 6 & 7. Now match the vocabulary words to their dictionary definitions. If there are words for which you cannot figure out the definition by contextual clues and by process of elimination, look them up in a dictionary.

   ___ 26. legacies   A. wanting the possessions of others
   ___ 27. chastisement   B. poisoned
   ___ 28. covetous   C. inherited money or goods
   ___ 29. exigent   D. punishment
   ___ 30. ensign   E. conceived
   ___ 31. engendered   F. critical moment
   ___ 32. envenomed   G. internal organs, especially intestines
   ___ 33. entrails   H. colors; flag carried by a company

ANSWER KEY - VOCABULARY
Julius Caesar

Act I	Act II	Act III	Acts IV & V
1. C	9. B	17. E	26. C
2. F	10. E	18. H	27. D
3. B	11. H	19. G	28. A
4. G	12. A	20. A	29. F
5. H	13. D	21. B	30. H
6. D	14. G	22. I	31. E
7. A	15. F	23. F	32. B
8. E	16. C	24 C	33. G
		25. D	

DAILY LESSONS

LESSONS ONE, TWO AND THREE

Objectives
1. To give students background information about Rome, the Roman Empire, and Julius Caesar
2. To give students practice using research materials
3. To give students practice finding, organizing, and presenting information

Activity 1

Take your class to your school library/media center. Divide your class into five groups, one group for each of the following topics:

Group One: Timeline history of Rome
Group Two: Geographical map(s) of the Roman Empire
Group Three: Biography of Julius Caesar
Group Four: Travelogue of modern Rome
Group Five: Culture, lifestyle, economics, government of modern Rome

Activity 2

Distribute the Research Project Assignment Sheet. Discuss the directions in detail and then give students time to work.

NOTE:

Students should use the remainder of the class period in Lesson One to do their research. Lesson Two's class time should be used to create the presentation for Lesson Three. In Lesson Three, students should make their presentations to the class

RESEARCH PROJECT ASSIGNMENT - *Julius Caesar*

PROMPT
    Before reading the play *Julius Caesar*, we are going to take a little time to explore Rome and the Roman Empire. This will give you some background information which will help you understand the play better, let you know what happened in the Roman Empire after the action of the play, and will show you how Rome is today.

ASSIGNMENT
    You have been divided into five groups, each with a different topic to explore. During this class period you will research your topic. In the next class period you will create a presentation about your topic to give to your classmates. In the class period after that you will actually make your presentations to the class.

REQUIREMENTS
1. Each group member must do research.
2. Each group member must keep a list of sources checked and summary of information found in those sources.
3. Each group member must make a written report. (See Writing Assignment 1)
4. Each group's presentation must be 8-10 minutes long.
5. Each group's presentation must include visual aids.

SUGGESTIONS

Group One: Divide your work among the group members, giving each member a segment of time to research. (For example, time before the Roman Empire, time during the Roman Empire, time between the fall of the Roman Empire and modern history, and modern history)
    Possible sources of information would be books, encyclopedias, periodicals, and films/videos.
    Use this class period to gather information. Take notes. In the next class period, bring materials to class to actually make a timeline. Use a roll of fax paper or shelf paper and colored markers to make the timeline. Another way to make it would be to use the overhead projector. Make your timeline in segments and place each segment on the overhead as you make your presentation. (Feel free to improvise to create a visually interesting timeline!)
    During your presentation, have each group member give a short report about his/her segment of Roman history. Coordinate the use of your timeline as a visual aid.

Group Two: There's an old saying, "Rome wasn't built in a day!" The Roman Empire developed, flourished, and declined over a period of hundreds of years. It is your job to show the geographical rise and fall of the Roman Empire.
    First, you have to research the history of the Roman Empire. A good encyclopedia article should give you a good outline of the periods in the history of the Roman Empire. Have one group member get the encyclopedia. Find the article, and have one group member read it to the group. One group member should take notes, noting the periods of the Empire. Then assign one

period of the Roman Empire's growth to each student in the group. All of this should take less than fifteen minutes. Use the rest of this class period for research. Each group member is looking for specific information about the geographical boundaries of the Roman Empire during the period he/she was assigned.

During the second class period, get together as a group to pool your information. Have each student give a brief report to the group. This is best done in chronological order. Spend the remainder of the second class period making your map(s). There are two ways to do this. The best way is to take a map of that part of the world and make several transparencies of it. Mark on the first transparency the area covered at the beginning of the era of the Roman Empire. Make each subsequent transparency showing the stages of growth (and retreat as the empire fell apart).

During the presentation, show the series of transparencies and give a brief explanation of the ways in which the land was acquired and lost.

Julius Caesar Research Project page 2

Group Three: Your task is twofold: to find biographical information about the man Julius Caesar and to find information about the play *Julius Caesar*. Divide your group in half. Half of you should work on the biography and half of you should work on information about the play. Make full use of your library's resources: books, periodicals, encyclopedias, films/videos, etc. Use the remainder of this first class period to do your research.

During the second class period, plan your presentation. The visual part of your presentation could be photos of Julius Caesar and pictures from a performance of the play, or you may have a group member dress up as Julius Caesar to talk about his life and the play William Shakespeare wrote about his assassination. You could make a family tree for Julius Caesar. Use your imagination to make your 10-minute presentation as interesting as possible.

Group Four: Some of your research can be done in the library, depending on the extent of the resources in your media center. Take a minute to ask your librarian/media specialist what visual materials about Rome exist at your school. If there are not many slides/videos or films/filmstrips, assign a member of your group to do library research. Other members should be assigned various video rental stores and travel agencies to contact to ask about the availability of visual information about Rome. If materials are available outside of your school, you need to plan and make arrangements for getting that information prior to your next class meeting.

In the second class period of this assignment, you should preview the information you have collected and create a way to make a ten-minute presentation using the information you have collected.

Group Five: Your assignment is to answer the question, "What is it like to live in Rome today?" Explore basic influences on the people of Rome: What kind of government do they have? What is the basis of their economy? What are current issues there? What do they wear? What do they eat? What is their educational system like? What influence does the church have on their lives? Don't limit yourselves to answering only these questions; they are examples of the kinds of questions your report should answer.

You might begin by brainstorming a list of topics to cover and assigning one (or more) topic(s) to each person in your group. That way, your research won't be duplicated. Be sure to use a variety of sources: books, periodicals, encyclopedias, etc. Use the remainder of this first class period to do your research.

In the second class period of this assignment, get together and pool your information. Decide how you will make your presentation, decide what visual aid(s) you will use and create them or make sure they are available for your use.

CONCLUDING NOTES

Remember your presentation is limited to ten minutes, and you don't have a whole lot of time for your research. That means you only have time to hit the most important highlights of your topic. We're not going for great depth in this assignment; rather, we are looking for an accumulation of a broad range of information. As you do your research and create your presentations, remember not to get too bogged down in minute details. They will eat up your time and energy. Skim articles and books to get to the most important parts. Use the table of contents to go right to the chapters that are most important to you. If one source doesn't seem to have what you need, don't keep looking in it hoping to find a little something; look for another source that may suit your objectives better.

If you find a video for your presentations that will suit the visual requirements of the assignment but doesn't really say what you want it to in the limited time you have, choose a five or ten minute segment of the video that has the most appropriate visuals. Turn the volume off and write your own script that gives all of your group's information.

WRITING ASSIGNMENT 1 - *Julius Caesar*

PROMPT
You have gathered information for your group's research project. This writing assignment is a part of the evaluation of your participation in your group's work. Your assignment is to write a report summarizing and evaluating your research.

PREWRITING
Most of your prewriting has already been done; you have it in the notes you took as you did your research. Gather your notes, review and organize them.

DRAFTING
Put your usual heading on your paper (name, date, class).
For each source you used, use this format:

NAME OF THE SOURCE YOU USED, Author (Date of Publication)

The first paragraph you write should give a brief summary of the contents of the source. What was it about?

The second paragraph you write about this source should give your analysis of the piece. Was it easy or difficult to understand? Why? Did the author cover the topic sufficiently? What did you think of it? Also make any other comments you choose to about your evaluation of the source.

The third paragraph you write about this source should tell how much you relied on this source for information. Was it your main source of information, did you use a few things from it, or was it a source you briefly looked at, decided wouldn't suit your objectives, and put aside?

PROMPT
When you finish the rough draft of your paper, ask a student who sits near you to read it. After reading your rough draft, he/she should tell you what he/she liked best about your work, which parts were difficult to understand, and ways in which your work could be improved. Reread your paper considering your critic's comments and make the corrections you think are necessary.

PROOFREADING
Do a final proofreading of your paper double-checking your grammar, spelling, organization, and the clarity of your ideas.

LESSON FOUR

Objectives
1. To complete the introduction of *Julius Caesar*
2. To distribute the materials students will use during this unit
3. To preview the study questions and vocabulary for Act I

Activity #1
Complete any presentations not finished in Lesson Three.

Activity #2
Distribute the materials students will use in this unit. Explain in detail how students are to use these materials.

Study Guides Students should read the study guide questions for each reading assignment prior to beginning the reading assignment to get a feeling for what events and ideas are important in the section they are about to read. After reading the section, students will (as a class or individually) answer the questions to review the important events and ideas from that section of the book. Students should keep the study guides as study materials for the unit test.

Vocabulary Prior to reading a reading assignment, students will do vocabulary work related to the section of the book they are about to read. Following the completion of the reading of the book, there will be a vocabulary review of all the words used in the vocabulary assignments. Students should keep their vocabulary work as study materials for the unit test.

Reading Assignment Sheet You need to fill in the reading assignment sheet to let students know by when their reading has to be completed. You can either write the assignment sheet up on a side blackboard or bulletin board and leave it there for students to see each day, or you can "ditto" copies for each student to have. In either case, you should advise students to become very familiar with the reading assignments so they know what is expected of them.

Extra Activities Center The Extra Activities portion of this unit contains suggestions for an extra library of related books and articles in your classroom as well as crossword and word search puzzles. Make an extra activities center in your room where you will keep these materials for students to use. (Bring the books and articles in from the library and keep several copies of the puzzles on hand.) Explain to students that these materials are available for students to use when they finish reading assignments or other class work early.

Books Each school has its own rules and regulations regarding student use of school books. Advise students of the procedures that are normal for your school.

Activity #3
> Assign various students to the parts to be spoken in Act I.

Activity #4
> Have students preview the study questions and do the vocabulary work for Act 1 of *Julius Caesar*. If students do not finish this assignment during this class period, they should complete it prior to the next class meeting.

LESSON FIVE

Objectives
> 1. To read Act 1
> 2. To give students practice reading orally
> 3. To evaluate students' oral reading

Activity
> Have students read Act 1 of *Julius Caesar* out loud in class. If you have not yet completed an oral reading evaluation for your students this marking period, this would be a good opportunity to do so. A form is included with this unit for your convenience.
>
> If students do not complete reading Act 1 in class, they should do so prior to your next class meeting.

ORAL READING EVALUATION - *Julius Caesar*

Name _____ Class____ Date _____

SKILL	EXCELLENT	GOOD	AVERAGE	FAIR	POOR
Fluency	5	4	3	2	1
Clarity	5	4	3	2	1
Audibility	5	4	3	2	1
Pronunciation	5	4	3	2	1
_____	5	4	3	2	1
_____	5	4	3	2	1

Total _____   Grade _____

Comments:

LESSON SIX

Objectives
    1. To review the main events and ideas from Act I
    2. To preview the study questions for Act II
    3. To familiarize students with the vocabulary in Act II
    4. To assign speaking parts for Act II

Activity #1
    Give students a few minutes to formulate answers for the study guide questions for Act I and then discuss the answers to the questions in detail. Write the answers on the board or overhead transparency so students can have the correct answers for study purposes. NOTE: It is a good practice in public speaking and leadership skills for individual students to take charge of leading the discussions of the study questions. Perhaps a different student could go to the front of the class and lead the discussion each day that the study questions are discussed during this unit. Of course, the teacher should guide the discussion when appropriate and be sure to fill in any gaps the students leave.

Activity #2
    Assign the speaking parts for students to read in Act II of *Julius Caesar*.

Activity #3
    Give students the remainder of the class time to preview the study questions for Act II of *Julius Caesar*, to do the related vocabulary work, and to practice their speaking parts.

LESSON SEVEN

Objectives
    1. To read Act II
    2. To give students practice reading orally
    3. To evaluate students' oral reading

Activity
    Have students read Act II of *Julius Caesar* out loud in class. Continue the oral reading evaluations. If students do not complete reading Act 1 in class, they should do so prior to your next class meeting.

LESSON EIGHT

Objectives
1. To review the main events and ideas from Act II
2. To preview the study questions for Act III
3. To familiarize students with the vocabulary in Act III
4. To assign speaking parts for Act III

Activity #1
   Give students a few minutes to formulate answers for the study guide questions for Act II and then discuss the answers to the questions in detail. Write the answers on the board or overhead transparency so students can have the correct answers for study purposes.

Activity #2
   Assign the speaking parts for students to read in Act III of *Julius Caesar*.

Activity #3
   Give students the remainder of the class time to preview the study questions for Act III of *Julius Caesar* to do the related vocabulary work and to practice their speaking parts.

LESSON NINE

Objectives
1. To read Act III
2. To give students practice reading orally
3. To evaluate students' oral reading

Activity
   Have students read Act III of *Julius Caesar* out loud in class. Continue the oral reading evaluations. If students do not complete reading Act III in class, they should do so prior to your next class meeting.

LESSON TEN

Objectives
1. To review the main events and ideas from Act III
2. To preview the study questions for Acts IV & V
3. To familiarize students with the vocabulary in Acts IV & V
4. To assign speaking parts for Acts IV & V

Activity #1
Give students a few minutes to formulate answers for the study guide questions for Act III and then discuss the answers to the questions in detail. Write the answers on the board or overhead transparency so students can have the correct answers for study purposes.

Activity #2
Assign the speaking parts for students to read in Acts IV & V of *Julius Caesar*.

Activity #3
Give students the remainder of the class time to preview the study questions for Acts IV & V of *Julius Caesar*, to do the related vocabulary work, and to practice their speaking parts.

LESSON ELEVEN

Objectives
1. To read Act IV
2. To give students practice reading orally
3. To evaluate students' oral reading

Activity
Have students read Act IV of *Julius Caesar* out loud in class. Continue the oral reading evaluations. If students do not complete reading Act IV in class, they should do so prior to your next class meeting.

LESSON TWELVE

Objectives
1. To read Act V
2. To give students practice reading orally
3. To evaluate students' oral reading

Activity
Have students read Act V of *Julius Caesar* out loud in class. Complete the oral reading evaluations if you have not yet done so.

LESSON THIRTEEN

Objectives
1. To review the main ideas and events from Act V
2. To prepare students for a class discussion of the play

Activity #1
Give students a few minutes to formulate answers for the study guide questions for Act V and then discuss the answers to the questions in detail. Write the answers on the board or overhead transparency so students can have the correct answers for study purposes.

Activity #2
Assign one of the Extra Discussion Questions to each of your students. Ideally, if you have a heterogeneous group, try to match the level of the question to the level of the student. Give quicker students more challenging questions, and easier questions to students who would be frustrated by too-difficult questions. Give students the remainder of the class period to answer their questions and prepare for the class discussion.

EXTRA WRITING ASSIGNMENTS/DISCUSSION QUESTIONS - *Julius Caesar*

<u>Interpretation</u>

1. Explain how the language of Shakespeare's play is different from the language we use today.

2. Give each act and scene a title.

3. Where is the climax of the play? Defend your answer.

4. What are the conflicts in the play, and how are they resolved?

<u>Critical</u>

5. Who is the best, most honorable character in the play? Justify your answer.

6. Are Brutus's actions believably motivated? Explain why or why not. Antony's?

7. Who is the worst, most corrupt character in the play? Justify your answer.

8. How does William Shakespeare's style of writing contribute to the value of the play?

9. Compare and contrast Antony and Brutus.

10. What things in *Julius Caesar* are ironic, and what effect does the use of irony have on our perception of the play?

11. Explain why the play *Julius Caesar* is a tragedy.

12. Compare and contrast Brutus and Cassius.

13. How is flattery used in the play?

14. What is the use of Lucius as a character in the play?

15. Are the characters in *Julius Caesar* stereotypes? If so, explain why William Shakespeare used stereotypes. If not, explain how the characters merit individuality.

Julius Caesar Extra Discussion Questions page 2

Personal Response

16. Would you have liked living in the Roman Empire? Why or why not?

17. Do you believe dreams have meaning in our daily lives? Why or why not?

18. Did you enjoy reading *Julius Caesar*? Why or why not?

19. Do you believe in ghosts? Why or why not?

20. Explain how someone could be "politically assassinated" (killing a person's political career without actually physically killing the person) in our modern times.

21. Who are some of America's greatest orators? What kinds of speeches do they give?

22. Discuss the role of the media (news, advertising, TV programming) in manipulating the general public today.

LESSON FOURTEEN

Objective
  To review all of the vocabulary work done in this unit

Activity
  Choose one (or more) of the vocabulary review activities listed below and spend your class period as directed in the activity. Some of the materials for these review activities are located in the Vocabulary Resource section of this unit.

VOCABULARY REVIEW ACTIVITIES

1. Divide your class into two teams and have an old-fashioned spelling or definition bee.

2. Give each of your students (or students in groups of two, three or four) a *Julius Caesar* Vocabulary Word Search Puzzle. The person (group) to find all of the vocabulary words in the puzzle first wins.

3. Give students a *Julius Caesar* Vocabulary Word Search Puzzle without the word list. The person or group to find the most vocabulary words in the puzzle wins.

4. Use a *Julius Caesar* Vocabulary Crossword Puzzle. Put the puzzle onto a transparency on the overhead projector (so everyone can see it), and do the puzzle together as a class.

5. Give students a *Julius Caesar* Vocabulary Matching Worksheet to do.

6. Divide your class into two teams. Use the *Julius Caesar* vocabulary words with their letters jumbled as a word list. Student 1 from Team A faces off against Student 1 from Team B. You write the first jumbled word on the board. The first student (1A or 1B) to unscramble the word wins the chance for his/her team to score points. If 1A wins the jumble, go to student 2A and give him/her a definition. He/she must give you the correct spelling of the vocabulary word which fits that definition. If he/she does, Team A scores a point, and you give student 3A a definition for which you expect a correctly spelled matching vocabulary word. Continue giving Team A definitions until some team member makes an incorrect response. An incorrect response sends the game back to the jumbled-word face off, this time with students 2A and 2B. Instead of repeating giving definitions to the first few students of each team, continue with the student after the one who gave the last incorrect response on the team. For example, if Team B wins the jumbled-word face-off, and student 5B gave the last incorrect answer for Team B, you would start this round of definition questions with student 6B, and so on. The team with the most points wins!

7. Have students write a story in which they correctly use as many vocabulary words as possible. Have students read their compositions orally! Post the most original compositions on your bulletin board!

LESSON FIFTEEN

Objectives
1. To discuss the play on a deeper than direct recall level
2. To examine some of the main themes in the play

Activity

Using students' answers to the Extra Discussion Questions (assigned in Lesson Thirteen) as a kickoff point, discuss the ideas presented by the Extra Discussion Questions.

LESSON SIXTEEN

Objectives
1. To give students the opportunity to practice writing to persuade
2. To check students' understanding of the causes and effects of the conspirators' assassination of Julius Caesar
3. To give the teacher the opportunity to evaluate students' writing

Activity

Distribute Writing Assignment 2. Discuss the directions in detail and give students this class period to work on the assignment.

WRITING ASSIGNMENT 2 - *Julius Caesar*

PROMPT
Knowing all you now know about Roman history, you are being transported back in time to the day of Caesar's assassination. Your assignment is to write an anonymous letter to the conspirators in which you persuade them not to carry out their plans.

PREWRITING
First, on a piece of paper jot down the reasons why the conspirators wanted to get rid of Julius Caesar. If you are going to persuade them against the actions they have planned, you need to fully understand what motivates them to do this thing in the first place. Keeping these things in mind and using all of your knowledge, write down at least three ideas to persuade the conspirators to cancel their plans. Jot down a few notes about your ideas to help explain them.

DRAFTING
Begin your letter in a letter format with the date and appropriate salutation.

Write an introductory paragraph in which you let the conspirators know that you know of their plans and to state your purpose for writing this letter.

In the body of your letter, write one paragraph stating and explaining each of your persuasive points (one paragraph for each point).

Write a concluding paragraph in which you summarize your points and make your final pleas.

Use an appropriate closing.

PROMPT
When you finish the rough draft of your paper, ask a student who sits near you to read it. After reading your rough draft, he/she should tell you what he/she liked best about your work, which parts were difficult to understand, and ways in which your work could be improved. Reread your paper considering your critic's comments and make the corrections you think are necessary.

PROOFREADING
Do a final proofreading of your paper double-checking your grammar, spelling, organization, and the clarity of your ideas.

LESSON SEVENTEEN

Objectives
1. To take a closer look at specific language/imagery used in the play
2. To discuss the further development of the themes of the play
3. To give students a chance to work together in small groups to exchange ideas and find information

Activity

Divide your class into eight groups - one group for each idea:
  (a) use of weather to set the tone
  (b) use of Caesar as a motivating force for the action of the novel
  (c) conflicts
  (d) use of the words "bleeding," "blood," and "bloody"
  (e) examples of honor, honesty, and nobility
  (f) treatment/manipulation of common people by the nobility
  (g) examples of tyranny/ambition
  (h) examples of reason versus emotion.

Allow the groups time to find specific examples of their topics in the play. The groups should assign so many acts per person to look for specific examples and write them down. Allow time for the group members to discuss their findings and come up with some intelligent ideas about their topics in the novel. The groups should appoint a spokesperson to report the group's thoughts.

LESSON EIGHTEEN

Objectives
1. To discuss the major themes in the play
2. To allow students time to review, compare and correct their notes

Activity #1
  Use the groups' work as a nucleus and a springboard for discussions about the major themes in the play. Call on individual group members by act(s) to give the examples they found of their theme in those acts. Jot them down briefly for students to copy into their notes. Ask the group spokesperson to give the group's thoughts about the theme development so far. Jot these down. Ask if anyone from the group has anything to add. Take the time to discuss each theme thoroughly with the class and be sure to allow time for students (either members of the group or other class members) to express their ideas or ask questions.

  NOTE: Having students report in this manner takes a little longer than having just one student from each group report, but it holds all group members accountable for their work.

Activity #2
  Allow any remaining time for students to review, compare and/or correct their notes.

LESSON NINETEEN

Objectives
1. To point out several important passages in Julius Caesar
2. To help students review some main ideas in Julius Caesar
3. To point out a few examples of Shakespeare's fine use of language
4. To give students personalized attention and feedback regarding their writing

Activity #1
Distribute the Quotations Worksheet. Students may either work on this assignment individually or in pairs, or you may wish to do the worksheet orally as a group (teacher's discretion). If it is not done orally, students should be given ample time to identify and explain the quotes given and then the class should discuss the explanations orally.

Activity #2
While students are formulating ideas about the quotations on the Quotations Worksheet, call individual students to your desk or some other private area in your classroom to hold short writing conferences with them. Use Writing Assignment #2 as a basis for your conference. There is a writing evaluation form included with this unit for your convenience if you want to use it to help structure your conferences.

LESSON TWENTY

Objectives
1. To give students a chance to apply things they learned in their writing conferences
2. To give students the opportunity to express their personal opinions
3. To give the teacher the opportunity to evaluate students' writing

Activity
Distribute Writing Assignment #3. Discuss the directions in detail and give students this class period to work on the assignment.

QUOTATIONS WORKSHEET - *Julius Caesar*

Identify and explain the following quotations from *Julius Caesar*.

1. These growing feathers plucked from Caesar's wing
   Will make him fly an ordinary pitch,
   Who else would soar above the view of men
   And keep us all in servile fearfulness. (I.i,77-80)

2. Beware the Ides of March. (I.ii,18)

3. But let not therefore my good friends be grieved --
   Among which number, Cassius, be you one --
   Nor construe any further my neglect
   Than that poor Brutus, with himself at war,
   Forgets the shows of love to other men. (I.ii,43-47)

4. I had as lief not be as live to be
   In awe of such a thing as I myself.
   I was born free as Caesar; so were you. (I.ii,95-97)

5. Yond Cassius has a lean and hungry look.
   He thinks too much, such men are dangerous. (I.ii,194-195)

6. And after this let Caesar seat him sure,
   For we will shake him, or worse days endure. (I.ii,325-326)

7. For I believe they are portentous things
   Unto the climate that they point upon. (I.iii,31-32)

8. But life, being weary of these worldly bars,
   Never lacks power to dismiss itself. (I.iii,96-97)

9. Three parts of him
   Is ours already, and the man entire
   Upon the next encounter yields him ours. (I.iii,154-156)

10. The abuse of greatness is when it disjoins
    Remorse from power (II.i,18-19)

11. And therefore think him as a serpent's egg
    Which hatched would as his kind grow mischievous,
    And kill him in the shell. (II.i,32-34)

12. No, not an oath. (II.i,114)

13. Let us be sacrificers, but not butchers, Caius. (II.i,166)

Julius Caesar Quotations Worksheet Page 2

14. Let's kill him boldly, but not wrathfully.
    Let's carve him as a dish fit for the gods,
    Not hew him as a carcass fit for hounds.
    And let our hearts, as subtle masters do,
    Stir up their servants to an act of rage
    And after seem to chide 'em. This shall make
    Our purpose necessary and not envious,
    Which so appearing to the common eyes,
    We shall be called purgers, not murderers.
    And for Mark Antony, think not of him.
    For he can do no more than Caesar's arm
    When Caesar's head is cut off. (II.i,172-183)

15.   O ye gods.
    Render me worthy of this noble wife! (II.i,302-303)

16. Thrice hath Calpurnia in her sleep cried out,
    "Help, ho! They murder Caesar!" (II.ii,2-3)

17. It seems to me most strange that men should fear,
    Seeing that death, a necessary end,
    Will come when it will come. (II.ii,35-37)

18.   Alas, my lord,
    Your wisdom is consumed in confidence. (II.ii,48-49)

19.   And so near will I be
    That your best friends shall wish I had been further. (II.ii,123-124)

20. If thou read this, O Caesar, thou mayst live;
    If not, the Fates with traitors do contrive. (II.iii,15-16)

21. I have a man's mind, but a woman's might. (II.iv,8)

22. Trebonius knows his time, for look you, Brutus,
    He draws Mark Antony out of the way. (III.i,24-25)

23. Hence! Wilt thou lift up Olympus? (III.i,73)

24. Liberty! Freedom! Tyranny is dead! (iii.i,78)

25. You know not what you do. Do not consent
    That Antony speak in his funeral. (iii.i,231-232)

26.   Censure me in your wisdom,
    and wake you senses, that you may the better judge. (III.ii,16-17)

27.   -- not that I loved Caesar less, but that I
    loved Rome more. (III.ii,22-23)

Julius Caesar Quotations Worksheet Page 3

28. Friends, Romans, countrymen, lend me your ears. (III.ii,78)

29. Yet Brutus says he was ambitious,
    And Brutus is an honorable man. (III.ii,87-88)

30. Let but the commons hear this testament --
    Which, pardon me, I do not mean to read -- (III.ii,135-136)

31. Now let it work. Mischief, thou art afoot,
    Take thou what course thou wilt. (III.ii,265-266)

32. It is no matter, his name's Cinna. Pluck
    but his name out of his heart, and turn him going. (III.iii,37-38)

33. These many then shall die, their names are pricked. (IV.i,1)

34. Do not talk of him
    But as a property. (IV.i,39-40)

35. You have done that you should be sorry for.
    There is no terror, Cassius, in your threats,
    For I am armed so strong in honesty
    That they pass by me as the idle wind
    Which I respect not. (IV.iii,63-69)

36. And we must take the current when it serves,
    Or lose our ventures. (IV.iii,222-223)

37. Why comest thou?
    To tell thee thou shalt see me at Philippi. (IV.iii,282-283)

38. But sufficeth that the day will end,
    And then the end is known. (V.i,125-126)

39. Caesar, thou art revenged,
    Even with the sword that killed thee. (V.iii,45-46)

40. O hateful error, melancholy's child,
    Why dost thou show to the apt thoughts of men
    The things that are not? (V.iii,67-69)

41. O Julius Caesar, thou are mighty yet! (V.iii,94)

Julius Caesar Quotations Worksheet Page 5

42.   Caesar, now be still.
    I killed not thee with half so good a will. (V.v,50-51)

43. This was the noblest Roman of them all.
    All the conspirators, save only he,
    Did that they did in envy of great Caesar.
    He only, in a general honest thought
    And common good to all, made one of them.
    His life was gentle, and the elements
    So mixed in him that Nature might stand up
    And say to all the world, "This was a man." (V.v,68-75)

WRITING EVALUATION FORM - *Julius Caesar*

Name _____ Date _____

Writing Assignment #1 for the *Julius Caesar* unit   Grade _____

Circle One For Each Item:

Grammar: corrections noted on paper

Spelling: corrections noted on paper

Punctuation: corrections noted on paper

Legibility: excellent   good   fair   poor

Strengths:

Weaknesses:

Comments/Suggestions:

WRITING ASSIGNMENT #3 - *Julius Caesar*

PROMPT
Brutus called Portia a "true and honorable wife." What is a "true and honorable wife (or husband)"? Write a composition in which you describe the most important characteristics of a true and honorable spouse.

PREWRITING
What characteristics did Portia have that made Brutus think of her as being true and honorable? Take a minute and jot down a list of characteristics that you think a true and honorable wife/husband would have. Next to each, make a few notes explaining how each characteristic would make a person true and honorable.

DRAFTING
Write an introductory paragraph in which you introduce the idea that Brutus thought Portia was a true and honorable wife and continue to make a statement about what characteristics you think a true and honorable wife/husband would have.

In the body of your composition, write one paragraph for each characteristic you have chosen. Within each paragraph explain how each characteristic would make a person true and honorable. Give examples and/or a thorough explanation.

Write a concluding paragraph taking into consideration all the characteristics you have mentioned above. You might make a statement about the likelihood of finding such a person.

PROMPT
When you finish the rough draft of your paper, ask a student who sits near you to read it. After reading your rough draft, he/she should tell you what he/she liked best about your work, which parts were difficult to understand, and ways in which your work could be improved. Reread your paper considering your critic's comments and make the corrections you think are necessary.

PROOFREADING
Do a final proofreading of your paper double-checking your grammar, spelling, organization, and the clarity of your ideas.

LESSON TWENTY-ONE

Objective
 To review the main ideas presented in *Julius Caesar*

Activity #1

 Choose one of the review games/activities included in the packet and spend your class period as outlined there. Some materials for these activities are located in the Unit Resource section of this unit.

Activity #2

 Remind students that the Unit Test will be in the next class meeting. Stress the review of the Study Guides and their class notes as a last-minute, brush-up review for homework.

REVIEW GAMES/ACTIVITIES - *Julius Caesar*

1. Ask the class to make up a unit test for Julius Caesar. The test should have 4 sections: matching, true/false, short answer, and essay. Students may use 1/2 period to make the test and then swap papers and use the other 1/2 class period to take a test a classmate has devised. (open book) You may want to use the unit test included in this packet or take questions from the students' unit tests to formulate your own test.

2. Take 1/2 period for students to make up true and false questions (including the answers). Collect the papers and divide the class into two teams. Draw a big tic-tac-toe board on the chalk board. Make one team X and one team O. Ask questions to each side, giving each student one turn. If the question is answered correctly, that students' team's letter (X or O) is placed in the box. If the answer is incorrect, no mark is placed in the box. The object is to get three marks in a row like tick-tack-toe. You may want to keep track of the number of games won for each team.

3. Take 1/2 period for students to make up questions (true/false and short answer). Collect the questions. Divide the class into two teams. You'll alternate asking questions to individual members of teams A & B (like in a spelling bee). The question keeps going from A to B until it is correctly answered, then a new question is asked. A correct answer does not allow the team to get another question. Correct answers are +2 points; incorrect answers are -1 point.

4. Have students pair up and quiz each other from their study guides and class notes.

5. Give students a *Julius Caesar* crossword puzzle to complete.

6. Divide your class into two teams. Use the *Julius Caesar* crossword words with their letters jumbled as a word list. Student 1 from Team A faces off against Student 1 from Team B. You write the first jumbled word on the board. The first student (1A or 1B) to unscramble the word wins the chance for his/her team to score points. If 1A wins the jumble, go to student 2A and give him/her a clue. He/she must give you the correct word which matches that clue. If he/she does, Team A scores a point, and you give student 3A a clue for which you expect another correct response. Continue giving Team A clues until some team member makes an incorrect response. An incorrect response sends the game back to the jumbled-word face off, this time with students 2A and 2B. Instead of repeating giving clues to the first few students of each team, continue with the student after the one who gave the last incorrect response on the team. For example, if Team B wins the jumbled-word face-off, and student 5B gave the last incorrect answer for Team B, you would start this round of clue questions with student 6B, and so on. The team with the most points wins!

UNIT TESTS

SHORT ANSWER UNIT TEST 1 - *Julius Caesar*

I. Matching/Identify

___ 1. Strato   A. Captured by Antony's soldiers

___ 2. Lucilius   B. Persuades Caesar to attend Senate meeting

___ 3. Octavius   C. First to stab Caesar

___ 4. Artemidorus   D. Organizes conspiracy & convinces Brutus to join

___ 5. Flavius   E. Holds Brutus' suicide sword

___ 6. Caesar   F. Wife of Brutus

___ 7. Casca   G. Plants forged letters

___ 8. Calpurnia   H. Beware the Ides of March

___ 9. Mark Antony   I. Distracts Caesar so murderers can kill him

___ 10. Portia   J. Joins and then leads conspiracy

___ 11. Trebonius   K. Emperor of Rome

___ 12. Decius   L. Caesar's wife

___ 13. Cinna   M. Heir of Julius Caesar; joins Antony

___ 14. Cassius   N. Leads Antony from Senate so he won't interfere

___ 15. Soothsayer   O. Breaks up crowd waiting to honor Caesar's triumph

___ 16. Brutus   P. Devoted follower of Caesar; defeats Brutus

___ 17. Metellus   Q. Gives Caesar a letter of warning

Julius Caesar Short Answer Unit Test 1 Page 2

II. Short Answer

1. Explain the difference between the views of Caesar held by Cassius and Brutus.

2. Why did Cassius want Brutus to join the conspiracy?

3. To what decision does Brutus come in his orchard?

4. Caesar yields to Calpurnia's wishes at first. Why does he change his mind and go to the Senate meeting?

5. What is ironic about the timing of Caesar's death?

6. What did Brutus say at the funeral?

7. What did Antony say at the funeral?

8. For what three reasons did Brutus want to lead his armies on to Philippi?

9. Why did Pindarus stab Cassius?

10. How does Brutus die?

Julius Short Answer Unit Test 1 Page 3

III. Composition

What is the point of *Julius Caesar*? When we read books, we usually come away from our reading experience a little richer, having given more thought to a particular aspect of life. What do you think William Shakespeare intended us to gain from reading his novel?

IV. Vocabulary

Listen to the vocabulary words and write them down. Go back later and fill in the correct definition for each word.

1.

2.

3.

4.

5.

6.

7.

8.

9.

10.

SHORT ANSWER UNIT TEST 2 - *Julius Caesar*

I. Matching

___ 1 Strato   A. Wife of Brutus

___ 2 Lucilius   B. Heir of Julius Caesar; joins Antony

___ 3 Octavius   C. Distracts Caesar so murderers can kill him

___ 4 Artemidorus   D. Emperor of Rome

___ 5 Flavius   E. Captured by Antony's soldiers

___ 6 Caesar   F. Holds Brutus' suicide sword

___ 7 Casca   G. Plants forged letters

___ 8 Calpurnia   H. Beware the Ides of March

___ 9 Mark Antony   I. First to stab Caesar

___ 10 Portia   J. Joins and then leads conspiracy

___ 11 Trebonius   K. Organizes conspiracy & convinces Brutus to join

___ 12 Decius   L. Caesar's wife

___ 13 Cinna   M. Leads Antony from Senate so he won't interfere

___ 14 Cassius   N. Persuades Caesar to attend Senate meeting

___ 15 Soothsayer   O. Breaks up crowd waiting to honor Caesar's triumph

___ 16 Brutus   P. Gives Caesar a letter of warning

___ 17 Metellus   Q. Devoted follower of Caesar; defeats Brutus

Julius Caesar Short Answer Unit Test 2 Page 2

II. Short Answer
Act I
1. Caesar clearly gives his thoughts about Cassius. What does he say?

2. Summarize Casca's explanation of why Caesar looked so sad.

3. Casca says, "For I believe they are portentous things/Unto the climate that they point upon." What does he mean?

4. Brutus is against including Cicero and against killing Mark Antony. Why?

5. Caesar yields to Calpurnia's wishes at first. Why does he change his mind and decide to go to the Senate meeting?

6. Why did Brutus and Cassius flee Rome?

7. What problem has developed between Cassius and Brutus? How is it resolved?

8. Why did Antony say Brutus was the "noblest Roman of them all"?

Julius Caesar Short Answer Unit Test 2 Page 3

III. Composition

Explain the role(s) of each of the following characters in *Julius Caesar*: Mark Antony, Brutus, Cassius, Casca, and Cinna. Write one complete paragraph about each character.

Julius Caesar Short Answer Unit Test 2 Page 4

IV. Vocabulary
    Listen to the vocabulary words and write them down. Go back later and fill in the correct definition for each word.

1.

2.

3.

4.

5.

6.

7.

8.

9.

10.

KEY: SHORT ANSWER UNIT TESTS - *Julius Caesar*

The short answer questions are taken directly from the study guides.
If you need to look up the answers, you will find them in the study guide section.

Answers to the composition questions will vary depending on your
class discussions and the level of your students.

For the vocabulary section of the test, choose ten of the
words from the vocabulary lists to read orally for your students.

The answers to the matching section of the test are below.

Answers to the matching section of the Advanced Short Answer Unit Test
are the same as for Short Answer Unit Test #2.

Test #1	Test #2
1. E	1. F
2. A	2. E
3. M	3. B
4. Q	4. P
5. O	5. O
6. K	6. D
7. C	7. I
8. L	8. L
9. P	9. Q
10. F	10. A
11. N	11. M
12. B	12. N
13. G	13. G
14. D	14. K
15. H	15. H
16. J	16. J
17. I	17. C

ADVANCED SHORT ANSWER UNIT TEST - *Julius Caesar*

I. Matching

___ 1. Strato   A. Wife of Brutus

___ 2. Lucilius   B. Heir of Julius Caesar; joins Antony

___ 3. Octavius   C. Distracts Caesar so murderers can kill him

___ 4. Artemidorus   D. Emperor of Rome

___ 5. Flavius   E. Captured by Antony's soldiers

___ 6. Caesar   F. Holds Brutus' suicide sword

___ 7. Casca   G. Plants forged letters

___ 8. Calpurnia   H. Beware the Ides of March

___ 9. Mark Antony   I. First to stab Caesar

___ 10. Portia   J. Joins and then leads conspiracy

___ 11. Trebonius   K. Organizes conspiracy & convinces Brutus to join

___ 12. Decius   L. Caesar's wife

___ 13. Cinna   M. Leads Antony from Senate so he won't interfere

___ 14. Cassius   N. Persuades Caesar to attend Senate meeting

___ 15. Soothsayer   O. Breaks up crowd waiting to honor Caesar's triumph

___ 16. Brutus   P. Gives Caesar a letter of warning

___ 17. Metellus   Q. Devoted follower of Caesar; defeats Brutus

Julius Caesar Advanced Short Answer Unit Test Page 2

II. Short Answer

1. What are the conflicts in the play, and how are they resolved?

2. Compare and contrast Antony and Brutus.

3. Explain why the play *Julius Caesar* is a tragedy.

4. Compare and contrast Brutus and Cassius.

Julius Caesar Advanced Short Answer Unit Test Page 3

5. What is the use of Lucius as a character in the play?

6. In what ways was the death of Julius Caesar predicted?

7. Compare and contrast Mark Antony's funeral oration with Brutus's.

8. Explain the role of tyranny/ambition in the play.

9. How does Shakespeare use reason versus emotion in the play?

Julius Caesar Advanced Short Answer Unit Test Page 4

III. Quotations: Explain the significance or importance of each of the following quotations from the play.

1. Beware the Ides of March. (I.ii,18)

2. Yond Cassius has a lean and hungry look.
   He thinks too much, such men are dangerous. (I.ii,194-195)

3. The abuse of greatness is when it disjoins
   Remorse from power (II.i,18-19)

4. Liberty! Freedom! Tyranny is dead! (iii.i,78)

5. You know not what you do. Do not consent
   That Antony speak in his funeral. (iii.i,231-232)

6.   -- not that I loved Caesar less, but that I
   loved Rome more. (III.ii,22-23)

7. Now let it work. Mischief, thou art afoot,
   Take thou what course thou wilt. (III.ii,265-266)

8. O Julius Caesar, thou are mighty yet! (V.iii,94)

Julius Caesar Advanced Short Answer Unit Test Page 5

IV. Vocabulary

Listen to the vocabulary words and write them down. Go back later and use them all in a short composition. The composition should relate in some way to *Julius Caesar*.

MULTIPLE CHOICE UNIT TEST 1 - *Julius Caesar*

I. Matching/Identify

___ 1. Strato   A. Captured by Antony's soldiers

___ 2. Lucilius   B. Persuades Caesar to attend Senate meeting

___ 3. Octavius   C. First to stab Caesar

___ 4. Artemidorus   D. Organizes conspiracy & convinces Brutus to join

___ 5. Flavius   E. Holds Brutus' suicide sword

___ 6. Caesar   F. Wife of Brutus

___ 7. Casca   G. Plants forged letters

___ 8. Calpurnia   H. Beware the Ides of March

___ 9. Mark Antony   I. Distracts Caesar so murderers can kill him

___ 10. Portia   J. Joins and then leads conspiracy

___ 11. Trebonius   K. Emperor of Rome

___ 12. Decius   L. Caesar's wife

___ 13. Cinna   M. Heir of Julius Caesar; joins Antony

___ 14. Cassius   N. Leads Antony from Senate so he won't interfere

___ 15. Soothsayer   O. Breaks up crowd waiting to honor Caesar's triumph

___ 16. Brutus   P. Devoted follower of Caesar; defeats Brutus

___ 17. Metellus   Q. Gives Caesar a letter of warning

Julius Caesar Multiple Choice Unit Test 1 Page 2

II. Multiple Choice

1. Explain the difference between the views of Caesar held by Cassius and Brutus.
    A. Cassius openly wants Caesar out of power. Brutus loves Caesar, but recognizes his flaws and thinks about the state of his countrymen.
    B. Cassius wants Caesar to stay in power. Brutus thinks Cassius would be a better leader, and wants to help him take over.
    C. Cassius wants Caesar out of power. Brutus agrees, but thinks Cassia would not be a good leader, either.
    D. Cassius thinks Caesar should share his power with Cassius, Brutus, and others. Brutus thinks the power should be divided equally among all of the countrymen.

2. At the end of Scene II in lines 312 - 326, Cassius makes plans. What plans does he make? Why?
    A. He is going to ask Casca and Brutus to have dinner with him the following evening to discuss what to do about Caesar.
    B. He plans to hold a reception in Caesar's honor to make amends with him.
    C. He is going to forge notes to Brutus from several citizens in order to help sway Brutus against Caesar.
    D. He is planning to kill Brutus.

3. Why does Cassius want Brutus to join the conspiracy?
    A. Brutus is well thought of by the people. If he supported the conspiracy the conspirators would be in better favor with the people following the assassination.
    B. Brutus has the best knowledge of the layout of the Capitol. It would be easy for him to plan a secret attack.
    C. Brutus has great influence over the soldiers. Cassius needs Brutus to direct them not to help Caesar.
    D. Brutus is very wealthy. They will need a lot of money to set up the new government.

4. Why doesn't Brutus want to swear an oath with the conspirators?
    A. He is planning to double-cross them later on.
    B. He thinks it is bad luck to swear an oath.
    C. He is afraid Lucius will overhear him and run to warn Caesar.
    D. He thinks a just cause needs no oath to bind the doers to their cause.

Julius Caesar Multiple Choice Unit Test 1 Page 3

5. For what reason does Metellus Cimber want Cicero to join the conspiracy?
    A. "... for his is given
       To sports, to wildness and much company.
       There is no fear in him..."
    B. "...his silver hairs
       Will purchase us a good opinion.
       And buy men's voices to commend our deeds..."
    C. "...we shall find of him
       A shrewd contriver..."
    D. "...thy master is wise and valiant Roman..."

6. Brutus is against including Cicero and against killing Mark Antony. Why?
    A. Cicero is a coward and Mark Antony can be persuaded to side with them.
    B. Cicero will not follow any plan started by someone else, and killing Mark Antony would be too bloody.
    C. Cicero may be a spy of Caesar's, and Mark Antony will not be a threat once Caesar is dead.
    D. Cicero wants the crown for himself, and if they kill Mark Antony, the Army will retaliate.

7. Of what does Calpurnia try to convince Caesar?
    A. Her dreams are omens of tragedy and he should not go to the Senate meeting.
    B. Her spies have told her that there is a plot against Caesar.
    C. There is going to be a terrible earthquake, and he should cancel the Senate meetings.
    D. He should let her and the other wives be present for his coronation.

8. Caesar yields to Calpurnia's wishes at first. Why does he change his mind and decide to go to the Senate meeting?
    A. His servants tell him the priests said it was alright for him to go.
    B. He knows that his army is strong and will protect him.
    C. He has seen a good luck omen in the sky. He thinks it is stronger than Calpurnia's dreams.
    D. Decius reinterprets Calpurnia's dream to entice Caesar to go to the meeting.

Julius Caesar Multiple Choice Unit Test 1 Page 4

9. What is ironic about the timing of Caesar's murder (in relation to the preceding events)?
    A. He is murdered just as he is reading the warning from Portia.
    B. He is destroyed just after proclaiming his magnificence and indestructibility.
    C. It occurs just after a great storm and earthquake.
    D. Brutus has changed his mind, but is not able to stop the others.

10. What did Brutus say to the people at the funeral?
    A. He told them the assassination was the only logical way to do the best thing for the people.
    B. He told them he would be a much better ruler than Caesar, and asked for their trust and support.
    C. He said he would divide Caesar's wealth among the people after the funeral.
    D. He criticized Caesar for being a cruel and evil ruler.

11. What did Antony say to the people at the funeral in his now famous "Friends, Romans, countrymen, lend me your ears" speech?
    A. He accuses the conspirators of treason and demands that they be put to death for Caesar's murder.
    B. He says the Caesar deserved to die, and the people should thank the conspirators.
    C. He contradicts the accusations made by the conspirators of treason and demands that they be put to death for Caesar's murder.
    D. He praises Caesar and asks that a memorial be built for him.

12. Why did Brutus and Cassius flee Rome?
    A. They had hidden Caesar's fortune and wanted to recover it.
    B. They want to get the army to put down the riot.
    C. They were following their wives, who had left the city earlier.
    D. Their lives were in danger after Antony's remarks at the funeral.

13. Which of these is not a reason that Brutus wants to lead his armies to Philippi?
    A. They can gather fresh forces as their march toward Philippi.
    B. The enemy is increasing and his army is at a high point ready to decline.
    C. They are on a "tide" of "fortune" and should strike while they are on a good tide.
    D. Antony is not expecting Brutus to go to Philippi. Brutus will have the element of surprise on his side.

14. How does Brutus die?
    A. Antony kills him in a fight.
    B. He kills himself with his sword.
    C. The ghost of Caesar frightened him to death.
    D. He is taken prisoner and one of the soldiers accidentally kills him.

Julius Caesar Multiple Choice Unit Test 1 Page 5

III. Quotations   Identify the speaker of the quotations.

A = Brutus   **B** = Soothsayer   **C** = Cassius   **D** = Caesar   **E** = Cinna   **F** = Antony

1. Beware the Ides of March. (I.ii,18)

2. The abuse of greatness is when it disjoins
   Remorse from power (II.i,18-19)

3. Let's kill him boldly, but not wrathfully.
   Let's carve him as a dish fit for the gods,
   Not hew him as a carcass fit for hounds.
   And let our hearts, as subtle masters do,
   Stir up their servants to an act of rage
   And after seem to chide 'em. This shall make
   Our purpose necessary and not envious,
   Which so appearing to the common eyes,
   We shall be called purgers, not murderers.
   And for Mark Antony, think not of him.
   For he can do no more than Caesar's arm
   When Caesar's head is cut off. (II.i,172-183)

4. Thrice hath Calpurnia in her sleep cried out,
   "Help, ho! They murder Caesar!" (II.ii,2-3)

5. Liberty! Freedom! Tyranny is dead! (iii.i,78)

6. You know not what you do. Do not consent
   That Antony speak in his funeral. (iii.i,231-232)

7.   -- not that I loved Caesar less, but that I
   loved Rome more. (III.ii,22-23)

8. Friends, Romans, countrymen, lend me your ears. (III.ii,78)

9. Now let it work. Mischief, thou art afoot,
   Take thou what course thou wilt. (III.ii,265-266)

10.   Caesar, thou art revenged,
    Even with the sword that killed thee. (V.iii,45-46)

Julius Caesar Multiple Choice Unit Test 1 Page 6

11.   Caesar, now be still.
    I killed not thee with half so good a will. (V.v,50-51)

12. This was the noblest Roman of them all.
    All the conspirators, save only he,
    Did that they did in envy of great Caesar.
    He only, in a general honest thought
    And common good to all, made one of them.
    His life was gentle, and the elements
    So mixed in him that Nature might stand up
    And say to all the world, "This was a man." (V.v,68-75)

Julius Caesar Multiple Choice Unit Test 1 Page 7

IV. Vocabulary

___ 1. Legacies   a. Poisoned

___ 2. Ingrafted   b. Critical moment

___ 3. Cogitations   c. Planted firmly

___ 4. Visage   d. Make an earnest request of

___ 5. Chastisement   e. Powerful; mighty

___ 6. Ensign   f. Foreboding

___ 7. Emulation   g. Temperament

___ 8. Exigent   h. Ill-will or spite

___ 9. Accoutered   i. Gladly

___ 10. Covetous   j. Inherited money or goods

___ 11. Entreat   k. Wanting the possessions of others

___ 12. Envenomed   l. Fully armed

___ 13. Puissant   m. Professional interpreters of omens

___ 14. Appeased   n. Punishment

___ 15. Fain   o. Envy; imitating

___ 16. Augurers   p. Interpret

___ 17. Construe   q. Face

___ 18. Mettle   r. Soothed; pacified

___ 19. Portentous   s. Colors; flag carried by a company

___ 20. Malice   t. Thoughts

MULTIPLE CHOICE UNIT TEST 2 - *Julius Caesar*

I. Matching

___ 1. Strato   A. Wife of Brutus

___ 2. Lucilius   B. Heir of Julius Caesar; joins Antony

___ 3. Octavius   C. Distracts Caesar so murderers can kill him

___ 4. Artemidorus   D. Emperor of Rome

___ 5. Flavius   E. Captured by Antony's soldiers

___ 6. Caesar   F. Holds Brutus' suicide sword

___ 7. Casca   G. Plants forged letters

___ 8. Calpurnia   H. Beware the Ides of March

___ 9. Mark Antony   I. First to stab Caesar

___ 10. Portia   J. Joins and then leads conspiracy

___ 11. Trebonius   K. Organizes conspiracy & convinces Brutus to join

___ 12. Decius   L. Caesar's wife

___ 13. Cinna   M. Leads Antony from Senate so he won't interfere

___ 14. Cassius   N. Persuades Caesar to attend Senate meeting

___ 15. Soothsayer   O. Breaks up crowd waiting to honor Caesar's triumph

___ 16. Brutus   P. Gives Caesar a letter of warning

___ 17. Metellus   Q. Devoted follower of Caesar; defeats Brutus

Julius Caesar Multiple Choice Unit Test 2 Page 2

II. Multiple Choice

1. Explain the difference between the views of Caesar held by Cassius and Brutus.
    - A. Cassius wants Caesar out of power. Brutus agrees but thinks Cassia would not be a good leader either.
    - B. Cassius wants Caesar to stay in power. Brutus thinks Cassius would be a better leader and wants to help him take over.
    - C. Cassius openly wants Caesar out of power. Brutus loves Caesar but recognizes his flaws and thinks about the state of his countrymen.
    - D. Cassius thinks Caesar should share his power with Cassius, Brutus, and others. Brutus thinks the power should be divided equally among all of the countrymen.

2.. At the end of Scene II in lines 312 - 326, Cassius makes plans. What plans does he make? Why?
    - A. He is going to ask Casca and Brutus to have dinner with him the following evening to discuss what to do about Caesar.
    - B. He plans to hold a reception in Caesar's honor to make amends with him.
    - C. He is planning to kill Brutus.
    - D. He is going to forge notes to Brutus from several citizens in order to help sway Brutus against Caesar.

3. Why does Cassius want Brutus to join the conspiracy?
    - A. Brutus has the best knowledge of the layout of the Capitol. It would be easy for him to plan a secret attack.
    - B. Brutus is well thought of by the people. If he supported the conspiracy, the conspirators would be in better favor with the people following the assassination.
    - C. Brutus has great influence over the soldiers. Cassius needs Brutus to direct them not to help Caesar.
    - D. Brutus is very wealthy. They will need a lot of money to set up the new government.

4. Why doesn't Brutus want to swear an oath with the conspirators?
    - A. He is planning to double-cross them later on.
    - B. He thinks a just cause needs no oath to bind the doers to their cause.
    - C. He is afraid Lucius will overhear him and run to warn Caesar.
    - D. He thinks it is bad luck to swear an oath.

Julius Caesar Multiple Choice Unit Test 2 Page 3

5. For what reason does Metellus Cimber want Cicero to join the conspiracy?
    A. "... for his is given
       To sports, to wildness and much company.
       There is no fear in him..."
    B. "...we shall find of him
       A shrewd contriver..."
    C. "...his silver hairs
       Will purchase us a good opinion.
       And buy men's voices to commend our deeds..."
    D. "...thy master is wise and valiant Roman..."

6. Brutus is against including Cicero and against killing Mark Antony. Why?
    A. Cicero is a coward and Mark Antony can be persuaded to side with them.
    B. Cicero wants the crown for himself, and if they kill Mark Antony, the Army will retaliate.
    C. Cicero may be a spy of Caesar's, and Mark Antony will not be a threat once Caesar is dead.
    D. Cicero will not follow any plan started by someone else, and killing Mark Antony would be too bloody.

7. Of what does Calpurnia try to convince Caesar?
    A. There is going to be a terrible earthquake, and he should cancel the Senate meetings.
    B. Her spies have told her that there is a plot against Caesar.
    C. Her dreams are omens of tragedy and he should not go to the Senate meeting.
    D. He should let her and the other wives be present for his coronation.

8. Caesar yields to Calpurnia's wishes at first. Why does he change his mind and decide to go to the Senate meeting?
    A. Decius reinterprets Calpurnia's dream to entice Caesar to go to the meeting.
    B. He knows that his army is strong and will protect him.
    C. He has seen a good luck omen in the sky. He thinks it is stronger than Calpurnia's dreams.
    D. His servants tell him the priests said it was alright for him to go.

9. What is ironic about the timing of Caesar's murder (in relation to the preceding events)?
    A. He is destroyed just after proclaiming his magnificence and indestructibility.
    B. He is murdered just as he is reading the warning from Portia.
    C. It occurs just after a great storm and earthquake.
    D. Brutus has changed his mind, but is not able to stop the others.

Julius Caesar Multiple Choice Unit Test 2 Page 4

10. What did Brutus say to the people at the funeral?
    A. He criticized Caesar for being a cruel and evil ruler.
    B. He told them he would be a much better ruler than Caesar, and asked for their trust and support.
    C. He said he would divide Caesar's wealth among the people after the funeral.
    D. He told them the assassination was the only logical way to do the best thing for the people.

11. What did Antony say to the people at the funeral in his now famous "Friends, Romans, countrymen, lend me your ears" speech?
    A. He accuses the conspirators of treason and demands that they be put to death for Caesar's murder.
    B. He says the Caesar deserved to die, and the people should thank the conspirators.
    C. He criticized Caesar for being a cruel and evil ruler.
    D. He praises Caesar and asks that a memorial be built for him.

12. Why did Brutus and Cassius flee Rome?
    A. They had hidden Caesar's fortune and wanted to recover it.
    B. Their lives were in danger after Antony's remarks at the funeral.
    C. They were following their wives, who had left the city earlier.
    D. They want to get the army to put down the riot.

13. Which of these is not a reason that Brutus wants to lead his armies to Philippi?
    A. They can gather fresh forces as their march toward Philippi.
    B. The enemy is increasing and his army is at a high point ready to decline.
    C. Antony is not expecting Brutus to go to Philippi. Brutus will have the element of surprise on his side.
    D. They are on a "tide" of "fortune" and should strike while they are on a good tide.

14. How does Brutus die?
    A. Antony kills him in a fight.
    B. The ghost of Caesar frightened him to death.
    C. He kills himself with his sword.
    D. He is taken prisoner and one of the soldiers accidentally kills him.

Julius Caesar Multiple Choice Unit Test 2 Page 5

III. Quotations   Identify the speaker of the quotations.

A = Cassius   B = Soothsayer   C = Brutus   D = Cinna   E = Antony   F = Caesar

1. Beware the Ides of March. (I.ii,18)

2. The abuse of greatness is when it disjoins
   Remorse from power (II.i,18-19)

3. Let's kill him boldly, but not wrathfully.
   Let's carve him as a dish fit for the gods,
   Not hew him as a carcass fit for hounds.
   And let our hearts, as subtle masters do,
   Stir up their servants to an act of rage
   And after seem to chide 'em. This shall make
   Our purpose necessary and not envious,
   Which so appearing to the common eyes,
   We shall be called purgers, not murderers.
   And for Mark Antony, think not of him.
   For he can do no more than Caesar's arm
   When Caesar's head is cut off. (II.i,172-183)

4. Thrice hath Calpurnia in her sleep cried out,
   "Help, ho! They murder Caesar!" (II.ii,2-3)

5. Liberty! Freedom! Tyranny is dead! (iii.i,78)

6. You know not what you do. Do not consent
   That Antony speak in his funeral. (iii.i,231-232)

7.   -- not that I loved Caesar less, but that I
   loved Rome more. (III.ii,22-23)

8. Friends, Romans, countrymen, lend me your ears. (III.ii,78)

9. Now let it work. Mischief, thou art afoot,
   Take thou what course thou wilt. (III.ii,265-266)

10.   Caesar, thou art revenged,
    Even with the sword that killed thee. (V.iii,45-46)

11.   Caesar, now be still.
    I killed not thee with half so good a will. (V.v,50-51)

12. This was the noblest Roman of them all.
    All the conspirators, save only he,
    Did that they did in envy of great Caesar.
    He only, in a general honest thought
    And common good to all, made one of them.
    His life was gentle, and the elements
    So mixed in him that Nature might stand up
    And say to all the world, "This was a man." (V.v,68-75)

Julius Caesar Multiple Choice Unit Test 2 Page 6

IV. Vocabulary

___ 1. Appertain   a. Belong to as a proper function or part

___ 2. Appeased   b. Soothed; pacified

___ 3. Chastisement   c. Interpret

___ 4. Malice   d. Envy; imitating

___ 5. Ingrafted   e. Temperament

___ 6. Consorted   f. Colors; flag carried by a company

___ 7. Puissant   g. Inherited money or goods

___ 8. Mettle   h. Planted firmly

___ 9. Fain   i. Punishment

___ 10. Covetous   j. Poisoned

___ 11. Strife   k. Omens

___ 12. Construe   l. Foreboding

___ 13. Ensign   m. Formal speech

___ 14. Portentous   n. Struggle, fight, or quarrel

___ 15. Oration   o. Wanting the possessions of others

___ 16. Legacies   p. Gladly

___ 17. Envenomed   q. Accompanied

___ 18. Prodigies   r. Face

___ 19. Emulation   s. Powerful; mighty

___ 20. Visage   t. Ill-will or spite

ANSWER SHEET - *Julius Caesar*
Multiple Choice Unit Tests

I. Matching	II. Multiple Choice	III. Quotes	IV. Vocabulary
1. ___	1. ___	1. ___	1. ___
2. ___	2. ___	2. ___	2. ___
3. ___	3. ___	3. ___	3. ___
4. ___	4. ___	4. ___	4. ___
5. ___	5. ___	5. ___	5. ___
6. ___	6. ___	6. ___	6. ___
7. ___	7. ___	7. ___	7. ___
8. ___	8. ___	8. ___	8. ___
9. ___	9. ___	9. ___	9. ___
10. ___	10. ___	10. ___	10. ___
11. ___	11. ___	11. ___	11. ___
12. ___	12. ___	12. ___	12. ___
13. ___	13. ___		13. ___
14. ___	14. ___		14. ___
15. ___			15. ___
16. ___			16. ___
17. ___			17. ___
			18. ___
			19. ___
			20. ___

ANSWER KEY MULTIPLE CHOICE UNIT TESTS – JULIUS CAESAR

Answers to Unit Test 1 are in the left column. Answers to Unit Test 2 are in the right column.

I. Matching	II. Multiple Choice	III. Quotes	IV. Vocabulary
1. E F	1. A C	1. B B	1. J A
2. A E	2. C D	2. A C	2. C B
3. M B	3. A B	3. A C	3. T I
4. Q P	4. D B	4. D F	4. Q T
5. O O	5. B C	5. E D	5. N H
6. K D	6. B D	6. C A	6. S Q
7. C I	7. A C	7. A C	7. O S
8. L L	8. D A	8. E E	8. B E
9. P Q	9. B A	9. E E	9. L P
10. F A	10. A D	10. C A	10. K O
11. N M	11. C A	11. A C	11. D N
12. B N	12. D B	12. F E	12. A C
13. G G	13. D C		13. E F
14. D K	14. B C		14. R L
15. H H			15. I M
16. J J			16. M G
17. I C			17. P J
			18. G K
			19. F D
			20. H R

UNIT RESOURCE MATERIALS

BULLETIN BOARD IDEAS - *Julius Caesar*

1. Leave a portion of the bulletin board for the students' best writing assignments.

2. Take one of the word search puzzles and draw it (enlarged) on the bulletin board. Write the clue words to find to one side. Invite students to take pens and find and circle the words in the time before and after class (or perhaps if they finish their work early).

3. Write several of the most significant quotations from the play onto the board on brightly colored paper.

4. Make a bulletin board listing the vocabulary words for this unit. As you complete sections of the play and discuss the vocabulary for each section, write the definitions on the bulletin board. (If your board is one students face frequently, it will help them learn the words.)

5. Make a travel or historical bulletin board about Rome. Your local travel agency might be a good place to find materials.

6. Post articles of criticism about *Julius Caesar*.

7. Make a bulletin board about Shakespeare. Place his picture in the middle of the board. Make playbills for each of his plays and post them around his picture.

8. Prepare the bulletin board with blank background paper and a title: SHAKESPEARE. As an introductory activity, have each student write on the board what comes to his/her mind when he/she hears the name "Shakespeare."

EXTRA ACTIVITIES

One of the difficulties in teaching a play is that all students don't read at the same speed. One student who likes to read may take the book home and finish it in a day or two. Sometimes a few students finish the in-class assignments early. The problem, then, is finding suitable extra activities for students.

The best thing I've found is to keep a little library in the classroom. For this unit on *Julius Caesar*, you might check out from the school library other related books and articles about Rome, Shakespeare, Elizabethan drama, world history, the Roman Empire, careers in government, other assassinations that have taken place throughout history, dreams/dream interpretations, or ghosts/the supernatural. Articles of criticism about the play would also be good to have on hand.

Other things you may keep on hand are puzzles. We have made some relating directly to *Julius Caeasr* you. Feel free to duplicate them for your class.

Some students may like to draw. You might devise a contest or allow some extra-credit grade for students who draw characters or scenes from *Julius Caesar*. Note, too, that if the students do not want to keep their drawings you may pick up some extra bulletin board materials this way. If you have a contest and you supply the prize (a CD or something like that perhaps), you could, possibly, make the drawing itself a non-refundable entry fee.

The pages which follow contain games, puzzles and worksheets. The keys, when appropriate, immediately follow the puzzle or worksheet. There are two main groups of activities: one group for the unit; that is, generally relating to the *Julius Caesar* text, and another group of activities related strictly to the *Julius Caesar* vocabulary.

Directions for these games, puzzles and worksheets are self-explanatory. The object here is to provide you with extra materials you may use in any way you choose.

MORE ACTIVITIES - *Julius Caesar*

1. Have students design a playbill for *Julius Caesar*.

2. Have students make a model or draw a map of the Globe theater.

3. Show a film version of *Julius Caesar* after you have completed reading the play in class. Have students evaluate the movie and compare/contrast it with the text.

4. Use some of the related topics noted earlier for an in-class library as topics for guest speakers.

5. Have students design a bulletin board (ready to be put up; not just sketched) for *Julius Caesar*.

6. Have groups of students act out scenes from the play.

7. Instead of making a whole production, assign a character to each student. Have that student design his/her own costume, memorize a short passage from the play, and recite the passage (in costume) in front of the class.

8. Hold a trial in which the conspirators are charged with treason and murder.

9. Have a Roman Empire day in your class. Have students dress up in Roman costumes, play music from the period, decorate your room as a Roman banquet hall, and have students each bring something for a meal of the time.

10. Have students plan a trip to Italy. They should research the cost of the trip, places to go and visit, accommodations and meals; everything they would need to actually make the trip. Students could write about things they would most like to see in Italy. You could have them write a descriptive essay as if they had taken the trip. You could get creative writing about the adventures they had in their travels. There are lots of possibilities!

11. "The abuse of greatness is when it disjoins/Remorse from power. . . ." Have students find current examples which show the meaning of this passage.

12. Take the time to analyze meter and rhyme of Shakespeare's writing.

13. Have students write a poem or song lyrics about the tragedy of *Julius Caesar*.

14. Do a mini-unit about persuasion: persuasive writing, advertising, speeches, etc.

WORD SEARCH - *Julius Caesar*

All words in this list are associated with *Julius Caesar*. The words are placed backwards, forward, diagonally, up and down. The included words are listed below the word searches.

```
M E T E L L U S U I C U L E P I D U S W O R D B
L I R R G G T V S O V A C A S U M C W U E C U K
M U G K L W C J P Y C M T R R I B L L Y I T H C
M E C H M F N L T A D T B O S E C L A I C C F N
N A S I T C O N S P I R A C Y R N S I H T H E H
P J R S L Y N R P M U T H V E C H U E U Y U D D
L C X C A I P R E T A I R D I T V R F N S D S Q
R O M E H L U K U C E E R O O U S S T R A T O B
L F T B V C A S S F I U R O P Z S D Z Y T T C B
V V J H H L K U C R M C S D R V V S X I H S E F
S L J Q P T I W V F X N S U W K U T T V U P R Y
A S R Q V N Y R M S R U Y T I R F I S I H I G P
H N M G O Q F R S G I R H C A L N U R V E O C T
J W T B C V M V A V G G I D W I I A J N R A H L
X H E O S A K K A N I N N R U L G P D R S X L T
C R O W N V O L U M N I U S U I S S A C W I F E
T O A T H Y F H C A P Y G J L Q J V A P W B F Q
```

ANTONY	DREAMS	MESSALA	ROME
BRUTUS	FLAVIUS	METELLUS	SENATE
BUTCHERS	FRIENDS	MIGHT	SOOTHSAYER
CASCA	FUNERAL	MIGHTY	STRATO
CASSIUS	HUNGRY	MISCHIEF	SWORD
CATO	JULIUS	MURDER	TITINIUS
CICERO	LEPIDUS	OATH	TREBONIUS
CINNA	LIGARIUS	OCTAVIUS	TYRANNY
CLITUS	LUCILIUS	PAPILIUS	VARRO
CONSPIRACY	LUCIUS	PINDARUS	VOLUMNIUS
CROWN	MAN	PORTIA	WIFE
DECIUS	MARCH	PUBLIUS	WILL

Crossword - *Julius Caesar*

Crossword Clues - *Julius Caesar*

ACROSS

2. Gives Caesar a letter of warning naming the conspirators
5. Soldier in army of Brutus & Cassius
7. Servant of Brutus
10. Render me worthy of this noble ____!
12. Let us be sacrificers, but not ____, Caius.
14. Organizes the conspiracy & gets Brutus to join
16. ... that Nature might stand up/And say to all the world, 'This was a ___'
17. Vows to follow Brutus
18. _____ Caesar
20. Plants the forged letter for Cassius
21. Liberty! Freedom! ____ is dead!
22. Caesar, now be still. I killed not thee with half so good a ____.
24. Devoted follower of Caesar; defeats Brutus
26. Reinterprets Calpurnia's dream and convinces Caesar to go to Senate
28. Beware the Ides of ___
30. Wife of Brutus
31. Friend & soldier to Brutus; refuses to hold Brutus's sword
33. Servant to Brutus
35. Captured by Antony's soldiers, mistaken for Brutus
36. Holds Brutus's suicide sword

DOWN

1. Antony offered Caesar one
3. ... not that I loved Caesar less, but that I loved ___ more
4. Brutus thinks a just cause needs no ___ to bind the doers to their cause
5. An agreement to perform together an illegal act
6. Officer; guards tent at Sardis
8. Reports Portia's death, discovers Cassius's body
9. Calpurnia tries to convince Caesar that her ___ are omens of tragedy
11. Tribune who breaks up crowd waiting to honor Caesar's triumph
12. Joins and then leads the conspiracy to kill Caesar
13. Caesar's wife
14. First to stab Caesar
15. Roman Senator to whom Casca talks on the eve of the assassination
19. I have a man's mind, but a woman's ___
20. Servant of Brutus; refused to kill Brutus
21. Takes Antony away from the assassination scene so he won't interfere
23. ___, Romans, countrymen, lend me your ears.
25. Heir of Julius Caesar
27. Caesar goes to this meeting
28. Distracts Caesar's attention so the conspirators can carry out their plan
29. Antony spoke at Caesar's
30. One of many who escort Caesar to the Senate meeting
32. Yond Cassius has a lean and ___ look
34. Caesar, thou are revenged, Even with the ___ that killed thee.

Crossword Answer Key - *Julius Caesar*

MATCHING QUIZ/WORKSHEET 1 - *Julius Caesar*

___ 1. LEPIDUS   A. Let us be sacrificers, but not ____, Caius.

___ 2. DECIUS   B. I have a man's mind, but a woman's ____.

___ 3. TITINIUS   C. Organizes the conspiracy & gets Brutus to join

___ 4. CONSPIRACY   D. Caesar, now be still. I killed not thee with half so good a ___.

___ 5. BUTCHERS   E. Yond Cassius has a lean and ___ look.

___ 6. TYRANNY   F. Officer, guards tent at Sardis

___ 7. SENATE   G. Servant to Cassius

___ 8. MIGHTY   H. Soldier in army of Brutus & Cassius

___ 9. PINDARUS   I. Reports Portia's death, discovers Cassius's body

___ 10. BRUTUS   J. Servant to Brutus

___ 11. HUNGRY   K. Servant of Brutus; refused to kill Brutus

___ 12. CATO   L. An agreement to perform together an illegal act

___ 13. LUCIUS   M. Vows to follow Brutus

___ 14. MIGHT   N. O Julius Caesar, thou art ____ yet.

___ 15. LIGARIUS   O. Reinterprets Calpurnia's dream and convinces Caesar to go to Senate

___ 16. CLITUS   P. Caesar goes to this meeting

___ 17. WILL   Q. Liberty! Freedom! ____ is dead!

___ 18. CASSIUS   R. Devoted follower of Caesar; defeats Brutus

___ 19. ANTONY   S. Joins with Octavius and Antony and is used by them

___ 20. MESSALA   T. Joins and then leads the conspiracy to kill Caesar

MATCHING QUIZ/WORKSHEET 2 - *Julius Caesar*

__ 1. METELLUS   A. Heir of Julius Caesar

__ 2. STRATO   B. Caesar, now be still. I killed not thee with half so good a ____.

__ 3. CALPURNIA   C. Tribune who breaks up crowd waiting to honor Caesar's triumph

__ 4. MAN   D. Joins with Octavius and Antony and is used by them

__ 5. LUCIUS   E. Holds Brutus's suicide sword

__ 6. TITINIUS   F. Caesar goes to this meeting

__ 7. TYRANNY   G. Antony offered Caesar one

__ 8. WILL   H. Distracts Caesar's attention so conspirators can carry out their plan

__ 9. MESSALA   I. Beware the Ides of ___

__ 10. FRIENDS   J. Liberty! Freedom! ____ is dead!

__ 11. LEPIDUS   K. ... that Nature might stand up/And say to all the world, 'This was a ___'

__ 12. CROWN   L. Officer, guards tent at Sardis

__ 13. PAPILIUS   M. Caesar, thou art revenged, Even with the ___ that killed thee.

__ 14. SWORD   N. Servant to Brutus

__ 15. VOLUMNIUS   O. ____, Romans, countrymen, lend me your ears.

__ 16. MARCH   P. Friend & soldier to Brutus; refuses to hold Brutus's sword

__ 17. FLAVIUS   Q. Brutus thinks a just cause needs no ___ to bind the doers to their cause

__ 18. SENATE   R. Reports Portia's death, discovers Cassius's body

__ 19. OATH   S. Caesar's wife

__ 20. OCTAVIUS   T. Wishes Cassius well in his 'enterprise'

KEY: MATCHING QUIZ/WORKSHEETS - *Julius Caesar*

Worksheet 1	Worksheet 2
1. S	1. H
2. O	2. E
3. F	3. S
4. L	4. K
5. A	5. N
6. Q	6. L
7. P	7. J
8. N	8. B
9. G	9. R
10. T	10. O
11. E	11. D
12. H	12. G
13. J	13. T
14. B	14. M
15. M	15. P
16. K	16. I
17. D	17. C
18. C	18. F
19. R	19. Q
20. I	20. A

JUGGLE LETTER REVIEW GAME CLUE SHEET - *Julius Caesar*

SCRAMBLED	WORD	CLUE
SECMIHFI	MISCHIEF	____, thou art afoot, Take thou what course thou wilt
UISCLU	LUCIUS	Servant to Brutus
MERO	ROME	... not that I loved Caesar less, but that I loved _____ more
USPIUBL	PUBLIUS	One of many who escort Caesar to the Senate meetings
ESTNAE	SENATE	Caesar goes to this meeting
IASRPDNU	PINDARUS	Servant to Cassius
LUUCLSII	LUCILIUS	Captured by Antony's soldiers, mistaken for Brutus
LERFANU	FUNERAL	Antony spoke at Caesar's
EUISDC	DECIUS	Reinterprets Calpurnia's dream and convinces Caesar to go to Senate
UISTITNI	TITINIUS	Officer, guards tent at Sardis
RCHMA	MARCH	Beware the Ides of _____
ANTNYRY	TYRANNY	Liberty! Freedom! _____ is dead!
SLELTMEU	METELLUS	Distracts Caesar's attention so conspirators can carry out their plan
OATSTR	STRATO	Holds Brutus's suicide sword
RDWSO	SWORD	Caesar, thou art revenged, Even with the _____ that killed thee.
TYHIGM	MIGHTY	O Julius Caesar, thou are _____ yet
UMERRD	MURDER	Help, ho! They _____ Caesar
ICTSLU	CLITUS	Servant of Brutus, refused to kill Brutus
ATOC	CATO	Soldier in army of Brutus & Cassius
GRLIASIU	LIGARIUS	Vows to follow Brutus
ROIESBNTU	TREBONIUS	Takes Antony away from the assassination scene so he won't interfere
NMA	MAN	___ that Nature might stand up/And say to all the world, 'This was a _____
RMSEAD	DREAMS	Calpurnia tries to convince Caesar that her _____ are omens of tragedy
RVORA	VARRO	Servant of Brutus
IUSCSSA	CASSIUS	Organizes the conspiracy and gets Brutus to join
CEMIIFSH	MISCHIEF	____, thou are afoot, Take thou what course thou wilt

Julius Caesar Juggle Letter Review Game Clue Sheet Continued

ATHO	OATH	Brutus thinks a just cause needs no ____ to bind the doers to their cause
STRBUU	BRUTUS	Joins and then leads the conspiracy to kill Caesar
ESAMLAS	MESSALA	Reports Portia's death, discovers Cassius's body
IEWF	WIFE	Render me worthy of this noble ____!
OCYCSPNIAR	CONSPIRACY	An agreement to perform together an illegal act
ILUSPPIA	PAPILIUS	Wishes Cassius well in his 'enterprise'
IMTGH	MIGHT	I have a man's mind, but a woman's ____
NDSRIEF	FRIENDS	____, Romans, countrymen, lend me your ears
NACIN	CINNA	Plants the forged letter for Cassius
LUIUSJ	JULIUS	____ Caesar
NNYATO	ANTONY	Devoted follower of Caesar; defeats Brutus
LUARNAPCI	CALPURNIA	Caesar's wife
ISDEPLU	LEPIDUS	Joins with Octavius and Antony and is used by them
RYHUGN	HUNGRY	Yond Cassius has a lean and ____ look
ITSORUMDERA	ARTEMIDORUS	Gives Caesar a letter of warning naming the conspirators
CSEHBRTU	BUTCHERS	Let us be sacrificers, but not ____, Cassius
RCICOE	CICERO	Roman Senator to whom Casca talks on the eve of the assassination
ACACS	CASCA	First to stab Caesar
WORNC	CROWN	Antony offered Caesar one
AITORP	PORTIA	Wife of Brutus

VOCABULARY RESOURCE MATERIALS

VOCABULARY WORD SEARCH - *Julius Caesar*

All words in this list are associated with *Julius Caesar* with an emphasis on the vocabulary words chosen for study in the text. The words are placed backwards, forward, diagonally, up and down. The included words are listed below.

```
M E Q Q R Y M N K N C Z V F G J T J R R S J G F
Y V N J N M K L R V G V D T C P Z A F F F Q J W
G N L V H Y F M D L Z D N G N Z U H M D J T X R
A U G M E N T E D E R E D N E G N E F A I N O W
S P D C J N S M F E M F U E U T I S Q F L T D K
E J P L O Q O S E E T H Q R S C N S T Z A I F F
T N W E B V E M S T K F E V T A O S N R R F C N
P C T B R I E I E R T R A O S S E N I E I H R E
G U P R C T T T N D S L F R R I N P S L W F N H
C R I A E S A O O C W B E W G A S O P O P D E W
H O G S A A I I X U T C A I R N T V C A R K R H
G E F H S T T N N N S K D S O G I I M A N T L E
L B C F A A F V E B L O D C E S N X O W Z X E M
T V N L E Q N G S H R M G P A Y M P J N P R S D
Y D U T H R I T H P T C O G I T A T I O N S D Q
F M G Q P X S W X F P Q E N B Q Q C T R Y S H N
E D E R E T U O C C A P O R T E N T O U S X F N
```

ACCOUTERED	COGITATIONS	ENTREAT	METTLE
APPEASED	CONSORTED	ENVENOMED	ORATION
APPERTAIN	CONSPIRATOR	EXIGENT	PORTENTOUS
AUGMENTED	CONSTRUE	FAIN	PRODIGIES
AUGURERS	COVETOUS	INGRAFTED	PUISSANT
BASE	EMULATION	LEGACIES	STRIFE
CHASTISEMENT	ENGENDERED	MALICE	VISAGE
COFFERS	ENSIGN	MANTLE	

Crossword 1 - *Julius Caesar* Vocabulary

Vocabulary Crossword Clues - *Julius Caesar*

ACROSS

2. Wanting the possessions of others
6. Professional interpreters of omens
8. Soldier in army of Brutus & Cassius
10. Punishment
13. Gladly
14. Made greater in size, quantity, or extent
15. Ill-will or spite
17. ... not that I loved Caesar less, but that I loved ___ more
18. Critical moment
20. Servant of Brutus
22. Friendliness; graciousness
25. Foreboding
26. Calpurnia tries to convince Caesar that her ____ are omens of tragedy
30. Brutus thinks a just cause needs no ___ to bind the doers to their cause
31. Fully armed
33. Caesar, now be still. I killed not thee with half so good a ____.
34. Poisoned
35. _____ Caesar
36. Caesar, thou art revenged, Even with the ___ that killed thee.

DOWN

1. Devoid of high values or ethics
3. Conceived
4. Formal speech
5. Struggle, fight, or quarrel
7. Colors; flag carried by a company
8. Thoughts
9. Public treasury
11. Make an earnest request of
12. Omens
14. Belong to as a proper function or part
16. Planted firmly
18. Envy
19. ... that Nature might stand up/And say to all the world, 'This was a ___'
21. Render me worthy of this noble ____!
23. Soothed; pacified
24. Antony spoke at Caesar's
26. Reinterprets Calpurnia's dream and convinces Caesar to go to Senate
27. Beware the Ides of ___
28. Holds Brutus's suicide sword
29. Plants the forged letter for Cassius
32. Antony offered Caesar one

Crossword 1 - *Julius Caesar* Vocabulary

	B							C	O	V	E	T	O	U	S					
	A	U	G	U	R	E	R	S			N		R		T		C	A	T	O
	S				N						G		A		R	O				C
	E		C	H	A	S	T	I	S	E	M	E	N	T		I		G		O
		P			I			N		N		I		F	A	I	N			F
		R		A	U	G	M	E	N	T	E	D		O		E		T		F
		O		P		N			R		E		N		M	A	L	I	C	E
		D		P		R	O	M	E		R				T		N			R
E	X	I	G	E	N	T			A		E		M		I		G		S	
M		G		R				T		D		V	A	R	R	O		R		
U		I		T			W			N			N		A					
L		E		A	F	F	A	B	I	L	I	T	Y		S		F			
A		S		I		P		F				F				T				
T			I	N		P	O	R	T	E	N	T	O	U	S		D	R	E	A	M	S
I		S		C		E					N		E		D		A			
O	A	T	H		I		A	C	C	O	U	T	E	R	E	D		C		R
N		R		N		S		R					R		W	I	L	L		C
		A		E	N	V	E	N	O	M	E	D			A			U		H
		T		A		D		W			J	U	L	I	U	S				
S	W	O	R	D				N												

VOCABULARY WORKSHEET 1 - *Julius Caesar*

___ 1. Fully armed
    a. Conspirator   b. Accoutered   c. Construe   d. Exigent

___ 2. Interpret
    a. Engendered   b. Exigent   c. Malice   d. Construe

___ 3. Wanting the possessions of others
    a. Covetous   b. Construe   c. Ingrafted   d. Strife

___ 4. Belong to as a proper function or part
    a. Visage   b. Mantle   c. Appertain   d. Fain

___ 5. Formal speech
    a. Portentous   b. Oration   c. Augurers   d. Envenomed

___ 6. Cloak
    a. Mantle   b. Malice   c. Oration   d. Coffers

___ 7. Made greater in size, quantity, or extent
    a. Emulation   b. Augmented   c. Ensign   d. Appeased

___ 8. One who plans with others to commit an illegal act
    a. Oration   b. Malice   c. Conspirator   d. Ensign

___ 9. Foreboding
    a. Malice   b. Base   c. Coffers   d. Portentous

___ 10. Envy; imitating
    a. Emulation   b. Portentous   c. Strife   d. Visage

___ 11. Friendliness; graciousness
    a. Appertain   b. Mantle   c. Affability   d. Conspirator

___ 12. Professional interpreters of omens
    a. Coffers   b. Augurers   c. Emulation   d. Appeased

___ 13. Poisoned
    a. Mantle   b. Chastisement   c. Envenomed   d. Covetous

___ 14. Ill-will or spite
    a. Oration   b. Prodigies   c. Mantle   d. Malice

___ 15. Devoid of high values or ethics
    a. Engendered   b. Coffers   c. Visage   d. Base

___ 16. Soothed; pacified
    a. Prodigies   b. Appeased   c. Puissant   d. Conspirator

___ 17. Gladly
    a. Exigent   b. Strife   c. Fain   d. Base

___ 18. Colors; flag carried by a company
    a. Mettle   b. Ensign   c. Visage   d. Cogitations

___ 19. Inherited money or goods
    a. Envenomed   b. Appeased   c. Legacies   d. Appertain

___ 20. Public treasury
    a. Coffers   b. Fain   c. Chastisement   d. Emulation

VOCABULARY WORKSHEET 2 - *Julius Caesar*

___ 1. Ingrafted   A. Planted firmly

___ 2. Affability   B. Interpret

___ 3. Augurers   C. Temperament

___ 4. Mettle   D. Professional interpreters of omens

___ 5. Conspirator   E. Critical moment

___ 6. Ensign   F. Formal speech

___ 7. Fain   G. Friendliness; graciousness

___ 8. Augmented   H. Powerful; mighty

___ 9. Covetous   I. Ill-will or spite

___ 10. Malice   J. Wanting the possessions of others

___ 11. Emulation   K. Inherited money or goods

___ 12. Legacies   L. Poisoned

___ 13. Construe   M. Gladly

___ 14. Puissant   N. One who plans with others to commit an illegal act

___ 15. Strife   O. Envy; imitating

___ 16. Visage   P. Face

___ 17. Appeased   Q. Made greater in size, quantity, or extent

___ 18. Envenomed   R. Soothed; pacified

___ 19. Exigent   S. Colors; flag carried by a company

___ 20. Oration   T. Struggle, fight, or quarrel

KEY: VOCABULARY WORKSHEETS - *Julius Caesar*

Worksheet 1	Worksheet 2
1. B	1. A
2. D	2. G
3. A	3. D
4. C	4. C
5. B	5. N
6. A	6. S
7. B	7. M
8. C	8. Q
9. D	9. J
10. A	10. I
11. C	11. O
12. B	12. K
13. C	13. B
14. D	14. H
15. D	15. T
16. B	16. P
17. C	17. R
18. B	18. L
19. C	19. E
20. A	20. F

VOCABULARY JUGGLE LETTER REVIEW GAME CLUES - *Julius Caesar*

SCRAMBLED	WORD	CLUE
GNUTMAEDE	AUGMENTED	Made greater in size, quantity, or extent
TNEMSTSCHEAI	CHASTISEMENT	Punishment
AIIFTLAFYB	AFFABILITY	Friendliness; graciousness
NSGENI	ENSIGN	Colors; flag carried by a company
ETTLEM	METTLE	Temperament
UTOINEMAL	EMULATION	Envy
ERAANPITP	APPERTAIN	Belong to as a proper function or part
TERANET	ENTREAT	Make an earnest request of
RSTDOOENC	CONSORTED	Accompanied
OTTNASCGOII	COGITATIONS	Thoughts
ESERGRUA	AUGERERS	Professional interpreters of omens
EMACIL	MALICE	Ill-will or spite
FAEGNRIDT	INGRAFTED	Planted firmly
RINAOTO	ORATION	Formal speech
GNXITEE	EXIGENT	Critical moment
SEBA	BASE	Devoid of high values or ethics
SENPTUORTO	PORTENTOUS	Foreboding
SRTEOUNC	CONSTRUE	Interpret
EGASVI	VISAGE	Face
REECOUATDC	ACCOUTERED	Fully armed
IORSEPGID	PRODIGIES	Omens
NTEMAL	MANTLE	Cloak
ESPDEAAP	APPEASED	Soothed; pacified
FISETR	STRIFE	Struggle, fight, or quarrel
NCRTORIOASP	CONSPIRATOR	One who plans with others to commit an illegal act
ENMDEVOEN	ENVENOMED	Poisoned
OSOTCEVU	COVETOUS	Wanting the possessions of others
DEDEGNENER	ENGENDERED	Conceived
SLEEACGI	LEGACIES	Inherited money or goods
SNINEG	ENSIGN	Colors; flag carried by a company
SAPTINUS	PUISSANT	Powerful; mighty
IFNA	FAIN	Gladly
RTANPIAPE	APPERTAIN	Belong to as a proper function or part
FBLIIFAAYT	AFFABILITY	Friendliness; graciousness

www.ingramcontent.com/pod-product-compliance
Lightning Source LLC
Chambersburg PA
CBHW051415070526
44584CB00023B/3445